Bootstrap

Jake Spurlock

D1441803

O'REILLY®

Beijing · Cambridge · Farnham · Köln · Sebastopol · Tokyo

Bootstrap

by Jake Spurlock

Copyright © 2013 Jake Spurlock. All rights reserved.

Printed in the United States of America.

Published by O'Reilly Media, Inc., 1005 Gravenstein Highway North, Sebastopol, CA 95472.

O'Reilly books may be purchased for educational, business, or sales promotional use. Online editions are also available for most titles (*http://my.safaribooksonline.com*). For more information, contact our corporate/institutional sales department: 800-998-9938 or *corporate@oreilly.com*.

Editors: Simon St. Laurent and Meghan Blanchette	**Indexer:** Judith McConville
Production Editor: Christopher Hearse	**Cover Designer:** Randy Comer
Copyeditor: BIM Publishing Services	**Interior Designer:** David Futato
Proofreader: Rachel Leach	**Illustrator:** Rebecca Demarest

May 2013:   First Edition

Revision History for the First Edition:

2013-05-07:   First release

See *http://oreilly.com/catalog/errata.csp?isbn=9781449343910* for release details.

ISBN: 978-1-449-34391-0

[LSI]

Table of Contents

Foreword

I was a software developer before Mac existed, so I remember how the tech industry reacted to it. For the most part, the community reacted with a fair amount of skepticism. The interesting thing is that the negative things people say about Bootstrap today sound exactly like the negative things people said about the Mac in 1984. And in both cases, the things that people didn't like were what made them important.

Apple realized that there is a set of things that all software has to do, so why shouldn't they all do them the same way? If they did, software would be easier to develop and debug, but more important—it would be easier to use. If there was only one way to create menus, then once a user learned how to use the menus of one app, he would already know how to use the menus of all others. The same is true with scrollbars, windows, the keyboard, the mouse, printing, and sound.

The reason programmers didn't like it, (and I was one of them) was that they took what we did and commoditized it. Further, there were limits to the one-size-fits-all approach. There were some apps that didn't take to the UI standards very well. What to do about them? Well, you adapted, that's what you did.

This is a well-known technical process called factoring. If you see yourself doing something over and over, do it one more time really well, work on the API so it's easy and flexible, and that's it. You never do it again. It's how you build ever-taller buildings out of software. What was the leading edge five years ago is baked into the operating system today. Progress. It's a wonderful thing!

The same patterns are observable in the Web. In fact, it's kind of sad how much of a repeat it is, how backward today's development environment is compared to the one envisioned by the Mac. But at least Bootstrap is out there doing the factoring. If I want to put up a menu, I can just use the code that creates menus. Sure, my menu looks like all the others, but that's a good thing for users. There is no need to learn a second or third way to use a menu.

That this is needed, desperately needed, is indicated by the incredible uptake of Bootstrap. I use it in all the server software I'm working on. And it shows through in the templating language I'm developing, so everyone who uses it will find it's "just there" and works any time you want to do a Bootstrap technique. Nothing to do; no libraries to include. It's as if it were part of the hardware. It's the same approach that Apple took with the Mac OS in 1984.

Like all important technologies, Bootstrap is "good enough" but not too good. In other words, the designers, Mark Otto and Jacob Thornton, could have factored more than they did. However, while they could have created something more compact and perhaps more elegant, it wouldn't have been nearly as approachable. The great thing about Bootstrap for a guy like me, who has been busy building software behind websites, is that it solves a whole bunch of problems that we all have when putting a user interface on those sites.

However, I think that will turn out to be just the beginning. I see the opportunity for Bootstrap to become an integral part of the Web—a toolkit that you can count on being present in every environment you work in. Further, someday, perhaps soon, designers will be able to plug in skins for Bootstrap that transform the appearance of a site without any modification to the code or to its styles or scripts. I don't see any limits to what can be done with Bootstrap. Rather than being a replacement for designers, it creates opportunities for designers to have more power and reach.

These days, part of the maturing process of any new technology is the release of its O'Reilly book. Now Bootstrap has one. The author, Jake Spurlock, a web developer, has been building sites with Bootstrap, has spoken at conferences about it, and he credits me for getting him started with a series of enthusiastic blog posts I wrote as I was discovering its power and elegance. Now, I can happily turn you over to Jake's able hands. He will show you how the Bootstrap magic works, so you too can help move the web development world forward.

—Dave Winer
editor, Scripting News, January 2013, New York

Preface

Bootstrap is a front-end framework for building responsive websites. Whether it is application frameworks, blogs, or other CMS applications, Bootstrap can be a good fit, as it can be as vanilla as you like. Its combination of HTML, CSS, and JavaScript make it easy to build robust sites without adding a lot of code. With a default grid system, layouts come together with ease, and the styling of buttons, navs, and tables make basic markup look great from the get-go. A dozen or so JavaScript plugins catapult you into adding interactive elements to your site.

Who This Book Is For

This book is mostly for people who have a good handle on HTML/CSS and JavaScript, and are curious about building responsive sites, adding the Bootstrap JavaScript plugins, or building sites faster by using this popular open source framework.

Who This Book Is Not For

This book is not for people who get all they need out of the Bootstrap online documentation. Like a lot of people, the online docs are where I got started—building my first site with Bootstrap 1.3 and then upgrading it to Bootstrap 1.4. After that, I built a big project with Bootstrap 2.0, and so on. If you are comfortable writing semantic HTML, then jumping into Bootstrap should be easy for you.

What This Book Will Do For You

If you have some background in writing HTML/CSS and JavaScript, this book will help you get off the ground writing some flexible code for responsive websites. In practical terms, the concepts and code syntax should come easily, as the book follows the patterns for writing semantic HTML and CSS.

How This Book Works

This book builds a site with Bootstrap, starting at the foundation of the project and the file structure, moving up through the grid system and layout types, and into HTML elements and styling like forms, tables, and buttons. Once the walls are up, we move into the aesthetic elements like navbars, breadcrumbs, and media objects. After that, we move on to the JavaScript elements, such as dropdowns, the carousel, and modals, that provide the interaction for a site.

Why I Wrote This Book

I'm not a Bootstrap expert hoping to create more Bootstrap experts to get a lot of work done.

I'm a developer and writer who encountered Bootstrap through a post on Dave Winer's blog, and I thought it would be cool to apply it to a new site that I was working on. I feel compelled to share some of what I've learned. I'm hoping that the path I followed will work for other people, probably with variations, and that a book written from a beginner's perspective (and vetted by experts) will help more people find and enjoy Bootstrap.

Other Resources

This book may not be the best way for you to learn Bootstrap. It all depends on what you want to learn and why.

If your primary interest is to get started building Bootstrap websites, the online documentation (*http://twitter.github.com/bootstrap/*) will likely suit you perfectly. The authors, Jacob Thornton and Mark Otto, have been meticulous in providing examples of the codebase, HTML code samples, and more to kickstart your project. It is top notch, and I've used it to gather the structure for this book.

If you want to contribute to the work of the open source project, you can submit pull requests or use the issue tracker on the GitHub project (*http://github.com/twitter/boot strap/*) for updates, downloads, documentation, and more.

Are You Sure You Want Bootstrap?

If you are looking for JavaScript plugins, or a CSS reset, Bootstrap may be overkill. If you aren't in love with some of the default interface elements, they can be overwritten easily or you can just strip out the associated tags. If you are looking for an easy way to build fast, responsive websites, Bootstrap is a great way to get going. I use it on all of my projects, and I'm really happy with it.

Conventions Used in This Book

The following typographical conventions are used in this book:

Italic

> Indicates new terms, URLs, email addresses, filenames, and file extensions.

`Constant width`

> Used for program listings, as well as within paragraphs to refer to program elements such as variable or function names, statements, and keywords.

`Constant width bold`

> Shows commands or other text that should be typed literally by the user.

`Constant width italic`

> Shows text that should be replaced with user-supplied values or by values determined by context.

> This icon signifies a tip, suggestion, or general note.

> This icon indicates a warning or caution.

Using Code Examples

The examples in this book are meant to teach basic concepts in small bites. While you may certainly borrow code and reuse it as you see fit, you won't be able to take the code of this book and build a stupendous application instantly (unless perhaps you have an unusual fondness for bacon and cats). You should, however, be able to figure out the steps you need to take to build a great website.

You can download the code from the Examples link on the book's page (*http://oreil.ly/bootstrap-web*).

This book is here to help you get your job done. In general, if this book includes code examples, you may use the code in this book in your programs and documentation. You do not need to contact us for permission unless you're reproducing a significant portion of the code. For example, writing a program that uses several chunks of code from this book does not require permission. Selling or distributing a CD-ROM of examples from O'Reilly books does require permission. Answering a question by citing this book and quoting example code does not require permission. Incorporating a significant amount of example code from this book into your product's documentation does require permission.

We appreciate, but do not require, attribution. An attribution usually includes the title, author, publisher, and ISBN. For example: "*Bootstrap*, by Jake Spurlock (O'Reilly). Copyright 2013 Jake Spurlock, 978-1-4493-4391-0."

If you feel your use of code examples falls outside fair use or the permission given above, feel free to contact us at *permissions@oreilly.com*.

Help This Book Grow

While I hope that you will enjoy reading this book and will learn from it, I also hope that you can contribute to helping other readers learn to use Bootstrap. You can help your fellow readers in a number of ways:

- If you find specific technical problems, bad explanations, or things that can be improved, please report them through the errata system (*http://oreil.ly/bootstrap-errata*).

- If you like (or don't like) the book, please leave reviews. The most visible places to do so are on Amazon.com (or its international sites) and at the O'Reilly page for the book (*http://oreil.ly/bootstrap-web*). Detailed explanations of what worked and what didn't work for you (and the broader target audience of programmers new to Bootstrap) are helpful to other readers and to me.

- If you find you have much more you want to say about Bootstrap, please consider sharing it, whether on the Web, in a book of your own, in training classes, or in whatever form you find easiest.

I'll update the book for errata and try to address issues raised in reviews. Even once the book is published, I may still add some extra pieces to it. If you purchased it as an ebook, you'll receive these updates for free until it's time for a whole new edition. I don't expect that new edition declaration to come quickly, however, unless the Bootstrap world changes substantially.

Hopefully this book will engage you enough to make you consider sharing.

Safari® Books Online

 *Safari Books Online* is an on-demand digital library that delivers expert content in both book and video form from the world's leading authors in technology and business.

Technology professionals, software developers, web designers, and business and creative professionals use Safari Books Online as their primary resource for research, problem solving, learning, and certification training.

Safari Books Online offers a range of product mixes and pricing programs for organizations, government agencies, and individuals. Subscribers have access to thousands of books, training videos, and prepublication manuscripts in one fully searchable database from publishers like O'Reilly Media, Prentice Hall Professional, Addison-Wesley Professional, Microsoft Press, Sams, Que, Peachpit Press, Focal Press, Cisco Press, John Wiley & Sons, Syngress, Morgan Kaufmann, IBM Redbooks, Packt, Adobe Press, FT Press, Apress, Manning, New Riders, McGraw-Hill, Jones & Bartlett, Course Technology, and dozens more. For more information about Safari Books Online, please visit us online.

How to Contact Us

Please address comments and questions concerning this book to the publisher:

O'Reilly Media, Inc.
1005 Gravenstein Highway North
Sebastopol, CA 95472
800-998-9938 (in the United States or Canada)
707-829-0515 (international or local)
707-829-0104 (fax)

We have a web page for this book, where we list errata, examples, and any additional information. You can access this page at *http://oreil.ly/bootstrap-web*.

To comment or ask technical questions about this book, send email to *bookquestions@oreilly.com*.

For more information about our books, courses, conferences, and news, see our website at *http://www.oreilly.com*.

Find us on Facebook: *http://facebook.com/oreilly*

Follow us on Twitter: *http://twitter.com/oreillymedia*

Watch us on YouTube: *http://www.youtube.com/oreillymedia*

Acknowledgments

Many thanks to Dave Winer for introducing me to Bootstrap in the first place, and to Simon St. Laurent for the opportunity to write this book. Detailed feedback from my friends Roseanne Fallin and Tony Quartorolo has made it possible; I hope that this book can get readers started on the right track. I would also like to thank Melissa Morgan for letting me take a few risks and develop the way that I like at *MAKE*.

In particular, thanks to my wonderful wife, Melissa, for putting up with me and encouraging me to finish. And thanks to my son, Rush, for understanding that I needed to "work" and to my daughter, Hailey, for the warm smiles and huge hugs. I love my family, and am so glad for everything they offer me.

CHAPTER 1

Bootstrap Scaffolding

What Is Bootstrap?

Bootstrap is an open source product from Mark Otto and Jacob Thornton who, when it was initially released, were both employees at Twitter. There was a need to standardize the frontend toolsets of engineers across the company. In the launch blog post, Mark Otto introduced the project like this:

> In the earlier days of Twitter, engineers used almost any library they were familiar with to meet front-end requirements. Inconsistencies among the individual applications made it difficult to scale and maintain them. Bootstrap began as an answer to these challenges and quickly accelerated during Twitter's first Hackweek. By the end of Hackweek, we had reached a stable version that engineers could use across the company.
>
> — Mark Otto
> *https://dev.twitter.com/*

Since Bootstrap launched in August 2011, it has taken off in popularity. It has evolved from being an entirely CSS-driven project to include a host of JavaScript plugins and icons that go hand in hand with forms and buttons. At its base, it allows for responsive web design and features a robust 12-column, 940px-wide grid. One of the highlights is the build tool on Bootstrap's website (*http://getbootstrap.com*), where you can customize the build to suit your needs, choosing which CSS and JavaScript features you want to include on your site. All of this allows frontend web development to be catapulted forward, building on a stable foundation of forward-looking design and development. Getting started with Bootstrap is as simple as dropping some CSS and JavaScript into the root of your site.

For someone starting a new project, Bootstrap comes with a handful of useful elements. Normally, when I start a project, I start with tools like Eric Meyer's Reset CSS (*http://meyerweb.com/eric/tools/css/reset/*) and get going on my web project. With Bootstrap, you just need to include the *bootstrap.css* CSS file and, optionally, the *bootstrap.js* Java-Script file into your website and you are ready to go.

Bootstrap File Structure

```
bootstrap/
        ├── css/
        │      ├── bootstrap.css
        │      ├── bootstrap.min.css
        ├── js/
        │      ├── bootstrap.js
        │      ├── bootstrap.min.js
        ├── img/
        │      ├── glyphicons-halflings.png
        │      ├── glyphicons-halflings-white.png
        └── README.md
```

The Bootstrap download includes three folders: css, js, and img. For simplicity, add these to the root of your project. Minified versions of the CSS and JavaScript are also included. It is not necessary to include both the uncompressed and the minified versions. For the sake of brevity, I use the uncompressed version during development and then switch to the compressed version in production.

Basic HTML Template

Normally, a web project looks something like this:

```
<!DOCTYPE html>
<html>
        <head>
                <title>Bootstrap 101 Template</title>
        </head>
        <body>
                <h1>Hello, world!</h1>
        </body>
</html>
```

With Bootstrap, we include the link to the CSS stylesheet and the JavaScript:

```
<!DOCTYPE html>
<html>
        <head>
                <title>Bootstrap 101 Template</title>
                <link href="css/bootstrap.min.css" rel="stylesheet">
        </head>
        <body>
                <h1>Hello, world!</h1>
                <script src="js/bootstrap.min.js"></script>
        </body>
</html>
```

Don't forget the HTML5 Doctype.

By including <!DOCTYPE html>, all modern browsers are put into standards mode.

Global Styles

With Bootstrap, a number of items come prebuilt. Instead of using the old reset block that was part of the Bootstrap 1.0 tree, Bootstrap 2.0 uses Normalize.css (*http://neco las.github.com/normalize.css/*), a project from Nicolas Gallagher that is part of the HTML5 Boilerplate (*http://html5boilerplate.com*). This is included in the *bootstrap.css* file.

In particular, the following default styles give special treatment to typography and links:

- `margin` has been removed from the body, and content will snug up to the edges of the browser window.
- `background-color: white;` is applied to the body.
- Bootstrap is using the `@baseFontFamily`, `@baseFontSize`, and `@baseLineHeight` attributes as our typographic base. This allows the height of headings and other content around the site to maintain a similar line height.
- Bootstrap sets the global link color via `@linkColor` and applies link underlines only on `:hover`.

Remember, if you don't like the colors or want to change a default, this can be done by changing the globals in any of the *.less* files. To do this, update the *scaffolding.less* file or overwrite colors in your own stylesheet.

Default Grid System

The default Bootstrap grid (see Figure 1-1) system utilizes 12 columns, making for a 940px-wide container without responsive features enabled. With the responsive CSS file added, the grid adapts to be 724px or 1170px wide, depending on your viewport. Below 767px viewports, such as the ones on tablets and smaller devices, the columns become fluid and stack vertically. At the default width, each column is 60 pixels wide and offset 20 pixels to the left. An example of the 12 possible columns is in Figure 1-1.

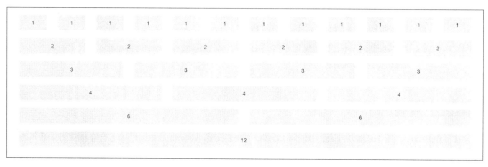

Figure 1-1. Default grid

Basic Grid HTML

To create a simple layout, create a container with a `<div>` that has a class of `.row` and add the appropriate amount of `.span*` columns. Since we have a 12-column grid, we just need the amount of `.span*` columns to equal 12. We could use a 3-6-3 layout, 4-8, 3-5-4, 2-8-2... we could go on and on, but I think you get the gist.

The following code shows `.span8` and `.span4`, which adds up to 12:

```
<div class="row">
  <div class="span8">...</div>
  <div class="span4">...</div>
</div>
```

Offsetting Columns

You can move columns to the right using the `.offset*` class. Each class moves the span over that width. So an `.offset2` would move a `.span7` over two columns (see Figure 1-2):

```
<div class="row">
  <div class="span2">...</div>
  <div class="span7 offset2">...</div>
</div>
```

Figure 1-2. Offset grid

Nesting Columns

To nest your content with the default grid, inside of a `.span*`, simply add a new `.row` with enough `.span*` that it equals the number of spans of the parent container (see Figure 1-3):

```
<div class="row">
  <div class="span9">
    Level 1 of column
    <div class="row">
      <div class="span6">Level 2</div>
      <div class="span3">Level 2</div>
    </div>
  </div>
</div>
```

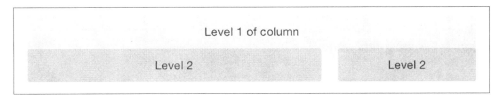

Figure 1-3. Nesting grid

Fluid Grid System

The fluid grid system uses percentages instead of pixels for column widths. It has the same responsive capabilities as our fixed grid system, ensuring proper proportions for key screen resolutions and devices. You can make any row "fluid" by changing `.row` to `.row-fluid`. The column classes stay exactly the same, making it easy to flip between fixed and fluid grids. To offset, you operate in the same way as the fixed grid system— add `.offset*` to any column to shift by your desired number of columns:

```
<div class="row-fluid">
  <div class="span4">...</div>
  <div class="span8">...</div>
</div>

<div class="row-fluid">
  <div class="span4">...</div>
  <div class="span4 offset2">...</div>
</div>
```

Nesting a fluid grid is a little different. Since we are using percentages, each `.row` resets the column count to 12. For example, if you were inside a `.span8`, instead of two `.span4` elements to divide the content in half, you would use two `.span6` divs (see

Figure 1-4). This is the case for responsive content, as we want the content to fill 100% of the container:

```
<div class="row-fluid">
  <div class="span8">
          <div class="row">
                  <div class="span6">...</div>
                  <div class="span6">...</div>
          </div>
  </div>
</div>
```

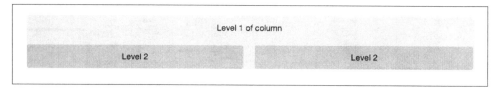

Figure 1-4. Nesting fluid grid

Container Layouts

To add a fixed-width, centered layout to your page, simply wrap the content in `<div class="container">...</div>`. If you would like to use a fluid layout but want to wrap everything in a container, use the following: `<div class="container-fluid">...</div>`. Using a fluid layout is great when you are building applications, administration screens, and other related projects.

Responsive Design

To turn on the responsive features of Bootstrap, you need to add a `<meta>` tag to the `<head>` of your web page. If you haven't downloaded the compiled source, you will also need to add the responsive CSS file. An example of required files looks like this:

```
<!DOCTYPE html>
<html>
      <head>
              <title>My amazing Bootstrap site!</title>
              <meta name="viewport" content="width=device-width,
          initial-scale=1.0">
              <link href="/css/bootstrap.css" rel="stylesheet">
              <link href="/css/bootstrap-responsive.css" rel="stylesheet">
      </head>
```

If you get started and find that the Bootstrap responsive features aren't working, make sure that you have these tags. The responsive features aren't added by default at this time because not everything needs to be responsive. Instead of encouraging developers to remove this feature, the authors of Bootstrap decided that it was best to enable it as needed.

What Is Responsive Design?

Responsive design is a method for taking all of the existing content that is on the page and optimizing it for the device that is viewing it. For example, the desktop not only gets the normal version of the website, but it might also get a widescreen layout, optimized for the larger displays that many people have attached to their computers. Tablets get an optimized layout, taking advantage of their portrait or landscape layouts. And then with phones, you can target their much narrower width. To target these different widths, Bootstrap uses CSS media queries to measure the width of the browser viewport and then, using conditionals, changes which parts of the stylesheets are loaded. Using the width of the browser viewport, Bootstrap can then optimize the content using a combination of ratios or widths, but it mostly relies on *min-width* and *max-width* properties.

At the core, Bootstrap supports five different layouts, each relying on CSS media queries. The largest layout has columns that are 70 pixels wide, contrasting with the 60 pixels of the normal layout. The tablet layout brings the columns to 42 pixels wide, and when narrower than that, each column goes fluid, meaning the columns are stacked vertically and each column is the full width of the device (see Table 1-1).

Table 1-1. Responsive media queries

Label	Layout width	Column width	Gutter width
Large display	1200px and up	70px	30px
Default	980px and up	60px	20px
Portrait tablets	768px and up	42px	20px
Phones to tablets	767px and below	Fluid columns, no fixed widths	
Phones	480px and below	Fluid columns, no fixed widths	

To add custom CSS based on the media query, you can either include all rules in one CSS file via the media queries below, or use entirely different CSS files:

```
/* Large desktop */
@media (min-width: 1200px) { ... }

/* Portrait tablet to landscape and desktop */
@media (min-width: 768px) and (max-width: 979px) { ... }

/* Landscape phone to portrait tablet */
@media (max-width: 767px) { ... }
```

```
/* Landscape phones and down */
@media (max-width: 480px) { ... }
```

For a larger site, you might want to divide each media query into a seperate CSS file. In the HTML file, you can call them with the `<link>` tag in the head of your document. This is useful for keeping file sizes smaller, but it does potentially increase the HTTP requests if the site is responsive. If you are using LESS to compile the CSS, you can have them all processed into one file:

```
<link rel="stylesheet" href="base.css" />
<link rel="stylesheet" media="(min-width: 1200px)" href="large.css" />
<link rel="stylesheet" media="(min-width: 768px) and (max-width: 979px)"
      href="tablet.css" />
<link rel="stylesheet" media="(max-width: 767px)" href="tablet.css" />
<link rel="stylesheet" media="(max-width: 480px)" href="phone.css" />
```

Helper classes

Bootstrap also includes a handful of helper classes for doing responsive development (see Table 1-2). Use these sparingly. A couple of use cases that I have seen involve loading custom elements based on certain layouts. Perhaps you have a really nice header on the main layout, but on mobile you want to pare it down, leaving only a few of the elements. In this scenario, you could use the `.hidden-phone` class to hide either parts or entire dom elements from the header.

Table 1-2. Media queries helper classes

Class	Phones	Tablets	Desktops
.visible-phone	Visible	Hidden	Hidden
.visible-tablet	Hidden	Visible	Hidden
.visible-desktop	Hidden	Hidden	Visible
.hidden-phone	Hidden	Visible	Visible
.hidden-tablet	Visible	Hidden	Visible
.hidden-desktop	Visible	Visible	Hidden

There are two major ways that you could look at doing development. The mantra that a lot of people are shouting now is that you should start with mobile, build to that platform, and let the desktop follow. Bootstrap almost forces the opposite, where you would create a full-featured desktop site that "just works."

If you are looking for a strictly mobile framework, Bootstrap is still a great resource.

CHAPTER 2

Bootstrap CSS

At the core of Bootstrap is a set of basic HTML elements that have been styled to allow for easy enhancement via classes and user styles.

Typography

Starting with typography, Bootstrap uses Helvetica Neue, Helvetica, Arial, and sans-serif in its default font stack. These are all standard fonts and are included as defaults on all major computers. If by chance these fonts don't exist, they fall back to `sans-serif` (the catchall) to tell the browser to use the default font for the browser. All body copy has the `font-size` set at 14 pixels, with the `line-height` set at 20 pixels. The `<p>` tag has a `margin-bottom` of 10 pixels, or half the `line-height`.

Headings

All six standard heading levels have been styled in Bootstrap (see Figure 2-1), with the `<h1>` at 36 pixels tall, and the `<h6>` down to 12 pixels (for reference, default body text is 14 pixels tall). In addition, to add an inline subheading to any of the headings, simply add `<small>` around any of the elements and you will get smaller text in a lighter color. In the case of the `<h1>`, the small text is 24 pixels tall, normal font weight (i.e., not bold), and gray instead of black:

```
h1 small {
    font-size:24px;
        font-weight:normal;
        line-height:1;
        color:#999;
        }
```

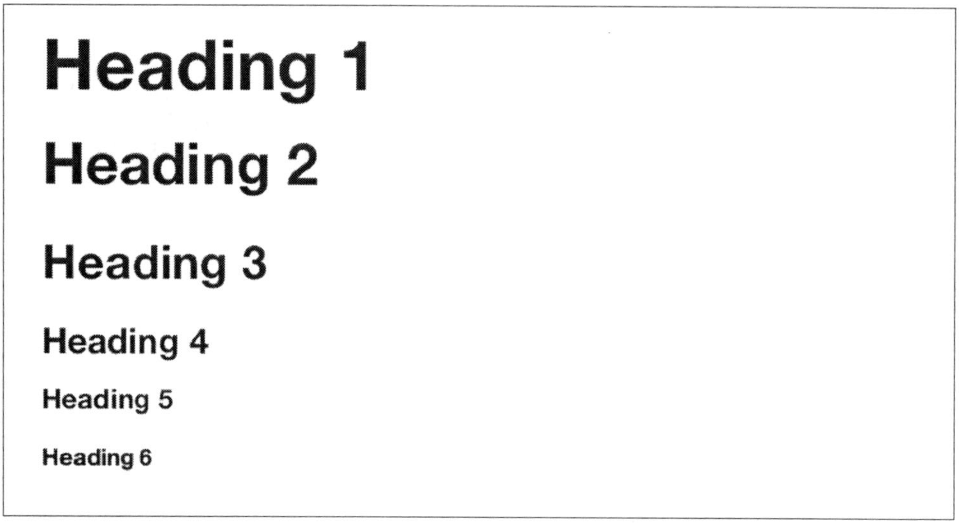

Heading 1
Heading 2
Heading 3
Heading 4
Heading 5
Heading 6

Figure 2-1. Headings

Lead Body Copy

To add some emphasis to a paragraph, add `class="lead"` (see Figure 2-2). This will give you larger font size, lighter weight, and a taller line height. This is generally used for the first few paragraphs in a section, but it can really be used anywhere:

```
<p class="lead">Bacon ipsum dolor sit amet tri-tip pork loin ball tip frankfurter
swine boudin meatloaf shoulder short ribs cow drumstick beef jowl.
Meatball chicken sausage tail, kielbasa strip steak turducken venison prosciutto.
Chuck filet mignon tri-tip ribeye, flank brisket leberkas. Swine
turducken turkey shank, hamburger beef ribs bresaola pastrami venison rump.</p>
```

Lead Example

Bacon ipsum dolor sit amet tri-tip pork loin ball tip frankfurter swine boudin meatloaf shoulder short ribs cow drumstick beef jowl. Meatball chicken sausage tail, kielbasa strip steak turducken venison prosciutto. Chuck filet mignon tri-tip ribeye, flank brisket leberkas. Swine turducken turkey shank, hamburger beef ribs bresaola pastrami venison rump.

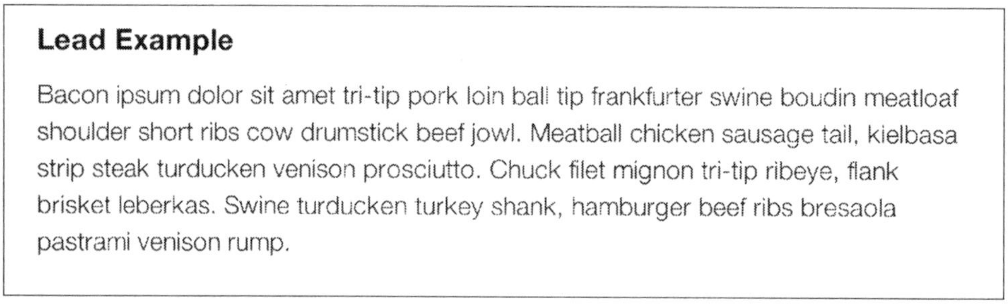

Figure 2-2. Lead body copy classes

Emphasis

In addition to using the <small> tag within headings, as discussed above, you can also use it with body copy. When <small> is applied to body text, the font shrinks to 85% of its original size.

Bold

To add emphasis to text, simply wrap it in a <strong> tag. This will add font-weight:bold; to the selected text.

Italics

For italics, wrap your content in the <em> tag. The term "em" derives from the word "emphasis" and is meant to add stress to your text.

 You might be thinking, why not just use the <b> or <i> tags instead of <em> or <strong>? In HTML5, <b> is meant to highlight words or phrases without conveying additional importance—for example, key terms or names—while <i> is mostly for voice, technical terms, internal dialogue, and so on. For more information about the semantic changes to <b> and <i>, check out W3.org's article (*http://www.w3.org/International/questions/qa-b-and-i-tags*).

Emphasis Classes

Along with <strong> and <em>, Bootstrap offers a few other classes that can be used to provide emphasis (see Figure 2-3). These could be applied to paragraphs or spans:

```
<p class="muted">This content is muted</p>
<p class="text-warning">This content carries a warning class</p>
<p class="text-error">This content carries an error class</p>
<p class="text-info">This content carries an info class</p>
<p class="text-success">This content carries a success class</p>
<p>This content has <em>emphasis</em>, and can be <strong>bold</strong></p>
```

Bootstrap Emphasis Classes

This content is muted

This content carries a warning class

This content carries an error class

This content carries an info class

This content carries a success class

This content has *emphasis*, and can be **bold**

Figure 2-3. Emphasis classes

Abbreviations

The HTML `<abbr>` element provides markup for abbreviations or acronyms, like WWW or HTTP (see Figure 2-4). By marking up abbreviations, you can give useful information to browsers, spell checkers, translation systems, or search engines. Bootstrap styles `<abbr>` elements with a light dotted border along the bottom and reveals the full text on hover (as long as you add that text to the `<abbr>` title attribute):

```
<abbr title="Real Simple Syndication">RSS</abbr>
```

RSS

Real Simple Syndication

Figure 2-4. Abbreviation example

Add `.initialism` to an `<abbr>` for a slightly smaller font size (see Figure 2-5):

```
<abbr title="rolling on the floor, laughing out loud">That joke had me ROTFLOL
</abbr>
```

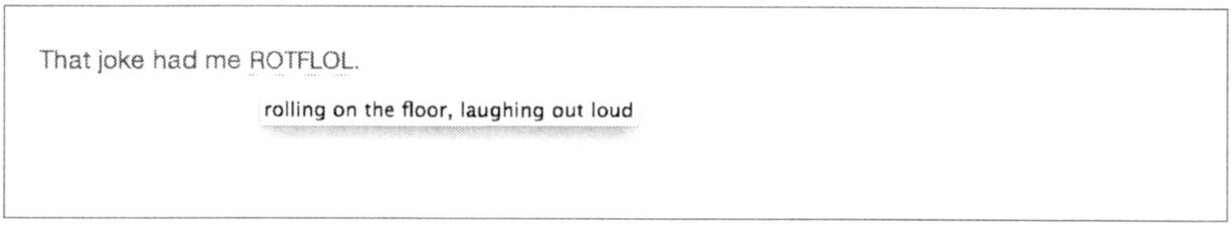

That joke had me ROTFLOL.

rolling on the floor, laughing out loud

Figure 2-5. Another abbreviation example

Addresses

Adding `<address>` elements to your page can help screen readers and search engines locate any physical addresses and phone numbers in the text (see Figure 2-6). It can also be used to mark up email addresses. Since the `<address>` defaults to `display:block;` you'll need to use `<br>` tags to add line breaks to the enclosed address text (e.g., to split the street address and city onto separate lines):

```
<address>
  <strong>O'Reilly Media, Inc.</strong><br>
  1005 Gravenstein HWY North<br>
  Sebastopol, CA 95472<br>
  <abbr title="Phone">P:</abbr> <a href="tel:+17078277000">(707) 827-7000</a>
</address>

<address>
  <strong>Jake Spurlock</strong><br>
  <a href="mailto:#">flast@oreilly.com</a>
</address>
```

O'Reilly Media, Inc.
1005 Gravenstein HWY North
Sebastopol, CA 95472
P: (707) 827-7000

Jake Spurlock
flast@oreilly.com

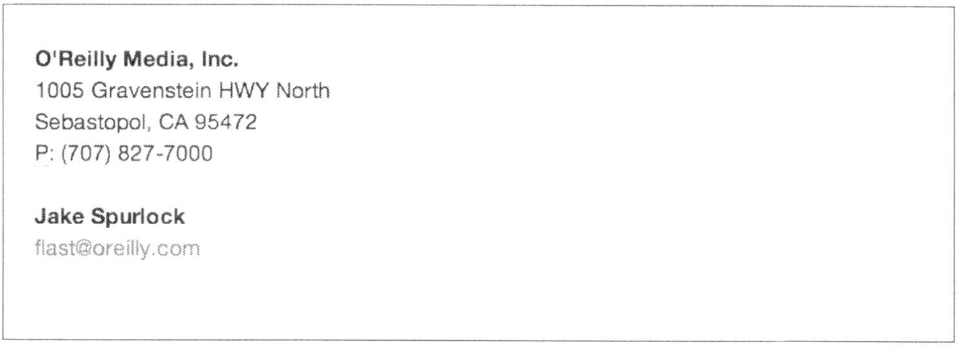

Figure 2-6. Address tag

Blockquotes

To add blocks of quoted text to your document—or for any quotation that you want to set apart from the main text flow—add the `<blockquote>` tag around the text. For best results, and for line breaks, wrap each subsection in a `<p>` tag. Bootstrap's default styling indents the text and adds a thick gray border along the left side. To identify the source of the quote, add the `<small>` tag, then add the source's name wrapped in a `<cite>` tag before closing the `</small>` tag:

```
<blockquote>
        <p>That this is needed, desperately needed, is indicated by the
    incredible uptake of Bootstrap. I use it in all the server software
    I'm working on. And it shows through in the templating language I'm
    developing, so everyone who uses it will find it's "just there" and
    works, any time you want to do a Bootstrap technique. Nothing to do,
    no libraries to include. It's as if it were part of the hardware.
    Same approach that Apple took with the Mac OS in 1984.</p>
        <small>Developer of RSS, <cite title="Source Title">Dave Winer</cite>
    </small>
</blockquote>
```

When you put it all together, you get something that looks like Figure 2-7.

> That this is needed, desperately needed, is indicated by the incredible uptake of Bootstrap. I use it in all the
> server software I'm working on. And it shows through in the templating language I'm developing, so everyone
> who uses it will find it's "just there" and works, any time you want to do a Bootstrap technique. Nothing to do,
> no libraries to include. It's as if it were part of the hardware. Same approach that Apple took with the Mac OS
> in 1984.
> — Developer of RSS, Dave Winer

Figure 2-7. Basic blockquote

 If you want a `<blockquote>` with content that is right aligned, add `.pull-right` to the tag. In addition to the right-aligned text, the entire blockquote is floated to the right. This creates nice pull-quotes in your content, as shown in Figure 2-8.

> Lorem ipsum dolor sit amet, consectetur adipisicing elit, sed do
> eiusmod tempor incididunt ut labore et dolore magna aliqua. Ut enim
> ad minim veniam, quis nostrud exercitation ullamco laboris nisi ut
> aliquip ex ea commodo consequat. Duis aute irure dolor in
> reprehenderit in voluptate velit esse cillum dolore eu fugiat nulla pariatur. Excepteur sint occaecat
> cupidatat non proident, sunt in culpa qui officia deserunt mollit anim id est laborum.
>
> This is just amazing.
> How cool is this?

Figure 2-8. Pull right blockquote

Lists

Bootstrap offers support and styling for the three main list types that HTML offers: ordered, unordered, and definition lists. An unordered list is a list that doesn't have any particular order and is traditionally styled with bullets.

Unordered list

If you have an ordered list that you would like to remove the bullets from, add `class="unstyled"` to the opening `<ul>` tag (see Figure 2-9):

```
<h3>Favorite Outdoor Activities</h3>
<ul>
        <li>Backpacking in Yosemite</li>
        <li>Hiking in Arches
                <ul>
                        <li>Delicate Arch</li>
                        <li>Park Avenue</li>
                </ul>
        </li>
        <li>Biking the Flintstones Trail</li>
</ul>
```

Favorite Outdoor Activities

- Backpacking in Yosemite
- Hiking in Arches
  - Delicate Arch
  - Park Avenue
- Biking the Flintstones Trail

Figure 2-9. Unordered list

 Personally, I hold a strong aversion to using the `<br>` tag. When I want a single-spaced line break, I place each line in an unstyled, unordered list. For example, if you want a condensed address box, like in Figure 2-6, you could code each line as `<li>`. In my mind, this is a more semantic way to mark up the text.

Ordered list

An ordered list is a list that falls in some sort of sequential order and is prefaced by numbers rather than bullets (see Figure 2-10). This is handy when you want to build a list of numbered items like a task list, guide items, or even a list of comments on a blog post:

```
<h3>Self-Referential Task List</h3>
<ol>
        <li>Turn off the internet.</li>
        <li>Write the book.</li>
        <li>... Profit?</li>
</ol>
```

Self-Referential Task List

1. Turn off the internet.
2. Right the book
3. ... Profit?

Figure 2-10. Ordered list

Definition list

The third type of list you get with Bootstrap is the definition list. The definition list differs from the ordered and unordered list in that instead of just having a block-level <li> element, each list item can consist of both the <dt> and the <dd> elements. <dt> stands for "definition term," and like a dictionary, this is the term (or phrase) that is being defined. Subsequently, the <dd> is the definition of the <dt>.

A lot of times in markup, you will see people using headings inside an unordered list. This works, but may not be the most semantic way to mark up the text. A better method would be creating a <dl> and then styling the <dt> and <dd> as you would the heading and the text (see Figure 2-11). That being said, Bootstrap offers some clean default styles and an option for a side-by-side layout of each definition:

```
<h3>Common Electronics Parts</h3>
<dl>
        <dt>LED</dt>
        <dd>A light-emitting diode (LED) is a semiconductor light source.</dd>
        <dt>Servo</dt>
        <dd>Servos are small, cheap, mass-produced actuators used for radio
    control and small robotics.</dd>
</dl>
```

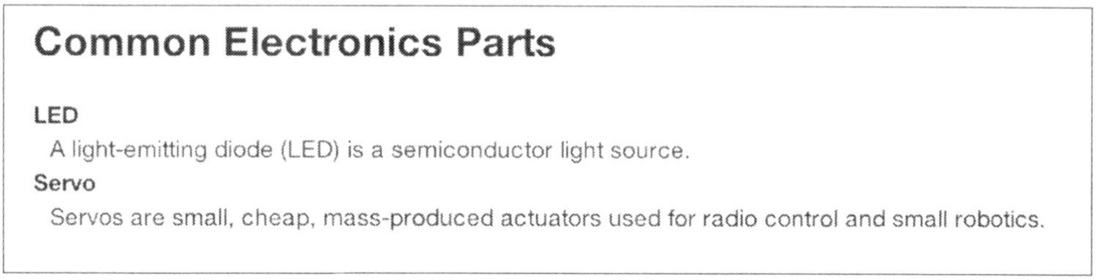

Common Electronics Parts

LED
  A light-emitting diode (LED) is a semiconductor light source.
Servo
  Servos are small, cheap, mass-produced actuators used for radio control and small robotics.

Figure 2-11. Definition list

To change the <dl> to a horizontal layout, with the <dt> on the left side and the <dd> on the right, simply add `class="dl-horizontal"` to the opening tag (see Figure 2-12).

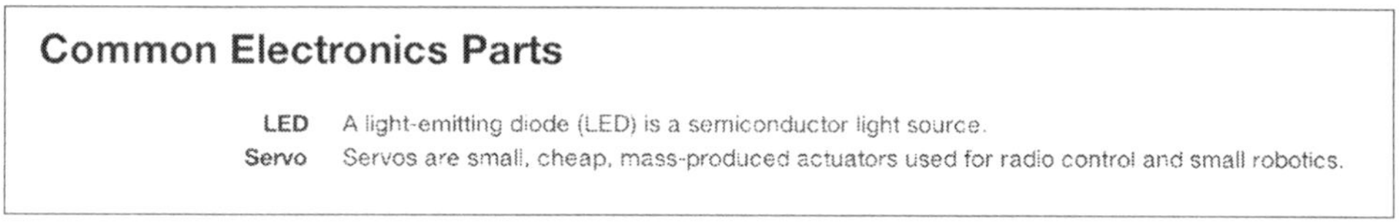

Common Electronics Parts

        LED   A light-emitting diode (LED) is a semiconductor light source.
        Servo   Servos are small, cheap, mass-produced actuators used for radio control and small robotics.

Figure 2-12. Horizontal definition list

 Horizontal description lists will truncate terms that are too long to fit in the left column with `text-overflow`. Additionally, in narrower viewports, they will automatically change to the default stacked layout.

Code

There are two different key ways to display code with Bootstrap. The first is the <code> tag and the second is the <pre> tag. Generally, if you are going to be displaying code inline, you should use the <code> tag. But if the code needs to be displayed as a standalone block element or if it has multiple lines, then you should use the <pre> tag:

```
<p>Instead of always using divs, in HTML5, you can use new elements like
<code>&lt;section&gt;</code>, <code>&lt;header&gt;</code>, and
<code>&lt;footer&gt;</code>. The html should look something like this:</p>
<pre>
  &lt;article&gt;
    &lt;h1&gt;Article Heading&lt;/h1&gt;
  &lt;/article&gt;
</pre>
```

Make sure that when you use the `<pre>` and `<code>` tags, you use the unicode variants for the opening and closing tags: `&lt;` and `&gt;`.

Tables

One of my favorite parts of Bootstrap is the nice way that tables are handled. I do a lot of work looking at and building tables, and the clean layout is a great feature that's included in Bootstrap right off the bat. Table 2-1 lists the various elements supported by Bootstrap.

Table 2-1. Table elements supported by Bootstrap

Tag	Description
`<table>`	Wrapping element for displaying data in a tabular format
`<thead>`	Container element for table header rows (`<tr>`) to label table columns
`<tbody>`	Container element for table rows (`<tr>`) in the body of the table
`<tr>`	Container element for a set of table cells (`<td>` or `<th>`) that appears on a single row
`<td>`	Default table cell
`<th>`	Special table cell for column (or row, depending on scope and placement) labels. Must be used within a `<thead>`
`<caption>`	Description or summary of what the table holds, especially useful for screen readers

If you want a nice, basic table style with just some light padding and horizontal dividers, add the base class of `.table` to any table (see Figure 2-13). The basic layout has a top border on all of the `<td>` elements:

```
<table class="table">
  <caption>...</caption>
  <thead>
    <tr>
      <th>...</th>
      <th>...</th>
    </tr>
  </thead>
  <tbody>
    <tr>
      <td>...</td>
      <td>...</td>
    </tr>
  </tbody>
</table>
```

Name	Phone Number	Rank
Kyle West	707-827-7001	Eagle
Davey Preston	707-827-7003	Eagle
Taylor Lemmon	707-827-7005	Eagle

Figure 2-13. Basic table class

Optional Table Classes

Along with the base table markup and the .table class, there are a few additional classes that you can use to style the markup. These four classes are: .table-striped, .table-bordered, .table-hover, and .table-condensed.

Striped table

By adding the .table-striped class, you will get stripes on rows within the <tbody> (see Figure 2-14). This is done via the CSS :nth-child selector, which is not available on Internet Explorer 7–8.

Name	Phone Number	Rank
Kyle West	707-827-7001	Eagle
Davey Preston	707-827-7003	Eagle
Taylor Lemmon	707-827-7005	Eagle

Figure 2-14. Striped table class

Bordered table

If you add the .table-bordered class, you will get borders surrounding every element and rounded corners around the entire table, as shown in Figure 2-15.

Name	Phone Number	Rank
Kyle West	707-827-7001	Eagle
Davey Preston	707-827-7003	Eagle
Taylor Lemmon	707-827-7005	Eagle

Figure 2-15. Bordered table class

Hover table

Figure 2-16 shows the `.table-hover` class. A light gray background will be added to rows while the cursor hovers over them.

Name	Phone Number	Rank
Kyle West	707-827-7001	Eagle
Davey Preston	707-827-7003	Eagle
Taylor Lemmon	707-827-7005	Eagle

Figure 2-16. Hover table class

Condensed table

If you add the `.table-condensed` class, as shown in Figure 2-17, row padding is cut in half to condense the table. This is useful if you want denser information.

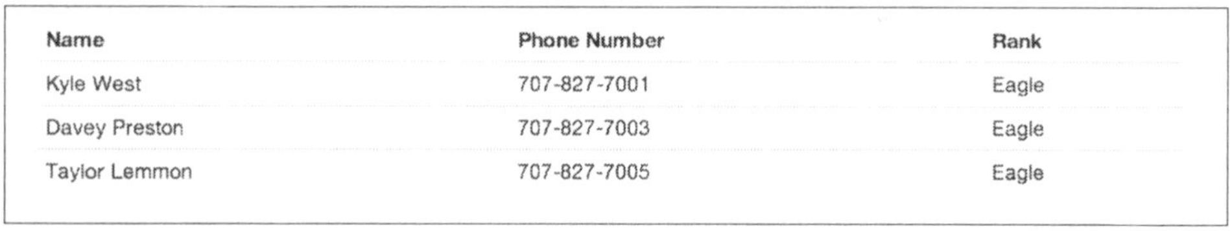

Name	Phone Number	Rank
Kyle West	707-827-7001	Eagle
Davey Preston	707-827-7003	Eagle
Taylor Lemmon	707-827-7005	Eagle

Figure 2-17. Condensed table class

Table Row Classes

The classes shown in Table 2-2 will allow you to change the background color of your rows (see Figure 2-18).

Table 2-2. Optional table row classes

Class	Description	Background color
`.success`	Indicates a successful or positive action.	Green
`.error`	Indicates a dangerous or potentially negative action.	Red
`.warning`	Indicates a warning that might need attention.	Yellow
`.info`	Used as an alternative to the default styles.	Blue

#	Product	Payment Taken	Status
1	TB - Monthly	01/04/2012	Approved
2	TB - Monthly	02/04/2012	Declined
3	TB - Monthly	03/04/2012	Pending
4	TB - Monthly	04/04/2012	Call in to confirm

Figure 2-18. Table row classes

Forms

Another one of the highlights of using Bootstrap is the ability to create forms with ease. As a web developer, styling forms is one of my least favorite tasks. Bootstrap makes it easy with the simple HTML markup and extended classes for different styles of forms.

The basic form structure comes with Bootstrap; there is no need to add any extra helper classes (see Figure 2-19). If you use the placeholder, keep in mind that it is only supported in newer browsers. In older browsers, no placeholder text will be displayed:

```
<form>
    <fieldset>
        <legend>Legend</legend>
            <label for="name">Label name</label>
            <input type="text" id="name"
        placeholder="Type something...">
            <span class="help-block">Example block-level help
             text here.</span>
            <label class="checkbox" for="checkbox">
                    <input type="checkbox" id="checkbox">
        Check me out
            </label>
        <button type="submit" class="btn">Submit</button>
    </fieldset>
</form>
```

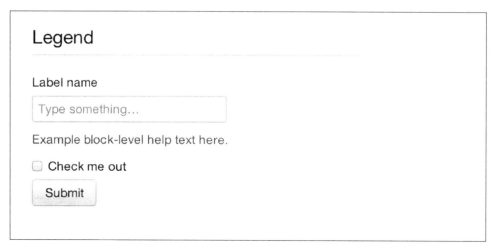

Figure 2-19. Basic form

Optional Form Layouts

With a few helper classes, you can dynamically update the layout of your form. Bootstrap comes with a few preset styles to choose from.

Search form

Add `.form-search` to the `<form>` tag, and then add `.search-query` to the `<input>` for an input box with rounded corners and an inline submit button (see Figure 2-20):

```
<form class="form-search">
  <input type="text" class="input-medium search-query">
  <button type="submit" class="btn">Search</button>
</form>
```

Figure 2-20. Search form

Inline form

To create a form where all of the elements are inline and labels are alongside, add the class `.form-inline` to the `<form>` tag (see Figure 2-21). To have the label and the input on the same line, use this inline form code:

```
<form class="form-inline">
        <input type="text" class="input-small" placeholder="Email">
        <input type="password" class="input-small" placeholder="Password">
```

```
            <label class="checkbox">
                    <input type="checkbox"> Remember me
            </label>
            <button type="submit" class="btn">Sign in</button>
    </form>
```

Figure 2-21. Inline form

Horizontal form

Bootstrap also comes with a prebaked horizontal form; this one stands apart from the others not only in the amount of markup, but also in the presentation of the form. Traditionally you'd use a table to get a form layout like the one shown in Figure 2-22, but Bootstrap manages to do it without using tables. Even better, if you're using the responsive CSS, the horizontal form will automatically adapt to smaller layouts by stacking the controls vertically.

To create a form that uses the horizontal layout, do the following:

- Add a class of .form-horizontal to the parent <form> element.
- Wrap labels and controls in a <div> with class .control-group.
- Add a class of .control-label to the labels.
- Wrap any associated controls in a <div> with class .controls for proper alignment.

Figure 2-22. Horizontal form

```
<form class="form-horizontal">
  <div class="control-group">
    <label class="control-label" for="inputEmail">Email</label>
```

```
        <div class="controls">
          <input type="text" id="inputEmail" placeholder="Email">
        </div>
      </div>
      <div class="control-group">
        <label class="control-label" for="inputPassword">Password</label>
        <div class="controls">
          <input type="password" id="inputPassword" placeholder="Password">
        </div>
      </div>
      <div class="control-group">
        <div class="controls">
          <label class="checkbox">
            <input type="checkbox"> Remember me
          </label>
          <button type="submit" class="btn">Sign in</button>
        </div>
      </div>
    </div>
  </form>
```

Supported Form Controls

Bootstrap natively supports the most common form controls. Chief among them are input, textarea, checkbox, radio, and select.

Inputs

The most common form text field is the input—this is where users will enter most of the essential form data (see Figure 2-23). Bootstrap offers support for all native HTML5 input types: text, password, datetime, datetime-local, date, month, time, week, number, email, URL, search, tel, and color:

```
<input type="text" placeholder="Text input">
```

Figure 2-23. Input

 Both input and textarea default to a nice blue glow when in the :active state.

Textarea

The `textarea` is used when you need multiple lines of input (see Figure 2-24). You'll find you mainly modify the `rows` attribute, changing it to the number of rows that you need to support (fewer rows = smaller box, more rows = bigger box):

```
<textarea rows="3"></textarea>
```

Figure 2-24. Both the :active default and the textarea

Checkboxes and radio buttons

Checkboxes and radio buttons are great when you want users to choose from a list of preset options (see Figure 2-25). When building a form, use `checkbox` if you want the user to select any number of options from a list. Use `radio` if you want to limit him to just one selection:

```
<label class="checkbox">
  <input type="checkbox" value="">
  Option one is this and that—be sure to include why it's great.
</label>

<label class="radio">
  <input type="radio" name="optionsRadios" id="optionsRadios1" value="option1"
  checked>
  Option one is this and that—be sure to include why it's great.
</label>
<label class="radio">
  <input type="radio" name="optionsRadios" id="optionsRadios2" value="option2">
  Option two can be something else, and selecting it will deselect option one
</label>
```

☐ Option one is this and that—be sure to include why it's great

○ Option one is this and that—be sure to include why it's great
◉ Option two can be something else and selecting it will deselect option one

Figure 2-25. Checkbox and radio buttons

If you want multiple checkboxes to appear on the same line together, add the `.inline` class to a series of checkboxes or radio buttons (see Figure 2-26):

```
<label for="option1" class="checkbox inline">
  <input id="option1" type="checkbox" id="inlineCheckbox1" value="option1"> 1
</label>
<label for="option2" class="checkbox inline">
  <input id="option2" type="checkbox" id="inlineCheckbox2" value="option2"> 2
</label>
<label for="option3" class="checkbox inline">
  <input id="option3" type="checkbox" id="inlineCheckbox3" value="option3"> 3
</label>
```

Figure 2-26. Inline checkboxes

Selects

A select is used when you want to allow the user to pick from multiple options, but by default it only allows one (see Figure 2-27). It's best to use `<select>` for list options with which the user is familiar, such as states or numbers. Use `multiple="multiple"` to allow the user to select more than one option. If you only want the user to choose one option, use `type="radio"`:

```
<select>
  <option>1</option>
  <option>2</option>
  <option>3</option>
  <option>4</option>
  <option>5</option>
</select>

<select multiple="multiple">
  <option>1</option>
  <option>2</option>
  <option>3</option>
  <option>4</option>
  <option>5</option>
</select>
```

Figure 2-27. Select

Extended Form Controls

In addition to the basic form controls listed in the previous section, Bootstrap offers a few other form components to complement the standard HTML form elements; for example, it lets you easily prepend and append content to inputs.

Prepended and appended inputs

By adding prepended and appended content to an input field, you can add common elements to the user's input (see Figure 2-28). For example, you can add the dollar symbol, the @ for a Twitter username, or anything else that might be common for your application interface. To add extra content before the user input, wrap the prepended input in a <div> with class .input-prepend. To append input, use the class .input-append. Then, within that same <div>, place your extra content inside a <span> with an .add-on class, and place the <span> either before or after the <input> element:

```
<div class="input-prepend">
  <span class="add-on">@</span>
  <input class="span2" id="prependedInput" type="text" placeholder="Username">
</div>
<div class="input-append">
  <input class="span2" id="appendedInput" type="text">
  <span class="add-on">.00</span>
</div>
```

Figure 2-28. Prepend and append

If you combine both of them, you simply need to add both the .input-prepend and .input-append classes to the parent <div> (see Figure 2-29):

```
<div class="input-prepend input-append">
  <span class="add-on">$</span>
  <input class="span2" id="appendedPrependedInput" type="text">
  <span class="add-on">.00</span>
</div>
```

Figure 2-29. Using both the append and prepend

Rather than using a `<span>`, you can instead use `<button>` with a class of `.btn` to attach (surprise!) a button or two to the input (see Figure 2-30):

```
<div class="input-append">
  <input class="span2" id="appendedInputButtons" type="text">
  <button class="btn" type="button">Search</button>
  <button class="btn" type="button">Options</button>
</div>
```

Figure 2-30. Attach multiple buttons to an input

If you are appending a button to a search form, you will get the same nice rounded corners that you would expect (see Figure 2-31):

```
<form class="form-search">
  <div class="input-append">
    <input type="text" class="span2 search-query">
    <button type="submit" class="btn">Search</button>
  </div>
  <div class="input-prepend">
    <button type="submit" class="btn">Search</button>
    <input type="text" class="span2 search-query">
  </div>
</form>
```

Figure 2-31. Append button to search form

Form Control Sizing

With the default grid system that is inherent in Bootstrap, you can use the `.span*` system for sizing form controls. In addition to the span column-sizing method, you can also use a handful of classes that take a relative approach to sizing. If you want the input to act as a block-level element, you can add `.input-block-level` and it will be the full width of the container element, as shown in Figure 2-32:

```
<input class="input-block-level" type="text" placeholder=".input-block-level">
```

Figure 2-32. Block-level input

Relative input controls

In addition to using `.span*` for input sizing, you can also use a few different class names (see Figure 2-33):

```
<input class="input-mini" type="text" placeholder=".input-mini">
<input class="input-small" type="text" placeholder=".input-small">
<input class="input-medium" type="text" placeholder=".input-medium">
<input class="input-large" type="text" placeholder=".input-large">
<input class="input-xlarge" type="text" placeholder=".input-xlarge">
<input class="input-xxlarge" type="text" placeholder=".input-xxlarge">
```

.input-mir

.input-small

.input-medium

.input-large

.input-xlarge

.input-xxlarge

Figure 2-33. Relative input controls

In future versions of Bootstrap, these input classes will be altered to match the button sizes. For example, `.input-large` will increase the padding and font size of an input.

Grid sizing

You can use any `.span` from `.span1` to `.span12` for form control sizing (see Figure 2-34):

```
<input class="span1" type="text" placeholder=".span1">
<input class="span2" type="text" placeholder=".span2">
<input class="span3" type="text" placeholder=".span3">
<select class="span1">
  ...
</select>
<select class="span2">
  ...
</select>
<select class="span3">
  ...
</select>
```

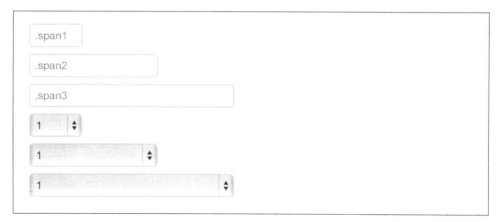

Figure 2-34. Span-sized inputs

If you want to use multiple inputs on a line, simply use the `.controls-row` modifier class to apply the proper spacing (see Figure 2-35). It floats the inputs to collapse the white space; sets the correct margins; and, like the `.row` class, clears the float:

```
<div class="controls">
  <input class="span5" type="text" placeholder=".span5">
</div>
<div class="controls controls-row">
  <input class="span4" type="text" placeholder=".span4">
  <input class="span1" type="text" placeholder=".span1">
```

```
</div>
...
```

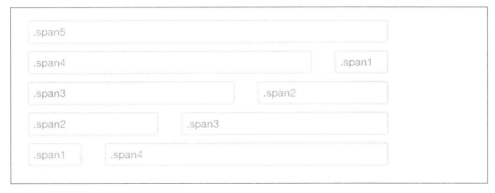

Figure 2-35. Control row

Uneditable text

If you want to present a form control without allowing the user to edit the input, simply add the class `.uneditable-input` (see Figure 2-36):

```
<span class="input-xlarge uneditable-input">Some value here</span>
```

Figure 2-36. Uneditable input

Form actions

When you place the form actions at the bottom of a `.horizontal-form`, the inputs will correctly line up with the floated form controls (see Figure 2-37):

```
<div class="form-actions">
  <button type="submit" class="btn btn-primary">Save changes</button>
  <button type="button" class="btn">Cancel</button>
</div>
```

Figure 2-37. Form controls

Help text

Bootstrap form controls can have either block or inline text that flows with the inputs (see Figure 2-38):

```
<input type="text"><span class="help-inline">Inline help text</span>
```

Figure 2-38. Inline help

To add a full width block of content, use the `.help-block` after the `<input>` (see Figure 2-39):

```
<input type="text"><span class="help-block">A longer block of help text that
breaks onto a new line and may extend beyond one line.</span>
```

Figure 2-39. Block help

Form Control States

In addition to the `:focus` state, Bootstrap offers styling for disabled inputs and classes for form validation.

Input focus

When an input receives `:focus` (i.e., a user clicks into the input or tabs onto it), the outline of the input is removed and a `box-shadow` is applied. I remember the first time that I saw this on Twitter's site; it blew me away, and I had to dig into the code to see how they did it. In WebKit, this is accomplished in the following manner:

```
input {
  -webkit-box-shadow: inset 0 1px 1px rgba(0, 0, 0, 0.075);
  -webkit-transition: box-shadow linear 0.2s;
}

input:focus {
  -webkit-box-shadow: inset 0 1px 1px rgba(0, 0, 0, 0.075), 0 0 8px
                      rgba(82, 168, 236, 0.6);
}
```

The `<input>` has a small inset `box-shadow`, which gives the appearance that the input sits lower than the page (see Figure 2-40). When `:focus` is applied, an 8px light blue border appears. The `webkit-transition` tells the browser to apply the effect in a linear manner over 0.2 seconds:

```
<input class="input-xlarge" id="focusedInput" type="text"
            value="This is focused...">
```

Figure 2-40. Focused input

Nice and subtle; a great effect.

Disabled input

If you need to disable an input, simply adding the `disabled` attribute will not only disable it; it will also change the styling and the mouse cursor when the cursor hovers over the element (see Figure 2-41):

```
<input class="input-xlarge" id="disabledInput" type="text"
            placeholder="Disabled input here..." disabled>
```

Figure 2-41. Disabled input

Validation states

Bootstrap includes validation styles for error, warning, info, and success messages (see Figure 2-42). To use, simply add the appropriate class to the surrounding `.control-group`:

```
<div class="control-group warning">
  <label class="control-label" for="inputWarning">Input with warning</label>
  <div class="controls">
    <input type="text" id="inputWarning">
    <span class="help-inline">Something may have gone wrong</span>
  </div>
</div>
<div class="control-group error">
  <label class="control-label" for="inputError">Input with error</label>
  <div class="controls">
    <input type="text" id="inputError">
```

```
    <span class="help-inline">Please correct the error</span>
  </div>
</div>
<div class="control-group success">
  <label class="control-label" for="inputSuccess">Input with success</label>
  <div class="controls">
    <input type="text" id="inputSuccess">
    <span class="help-inline">Woohoo!</span>
  </div>
</div>
```

Input with warning		Something may have gone wrong
Input with error		Please correct the error
Input with info		Username is taken
Input with success		Woohoo!

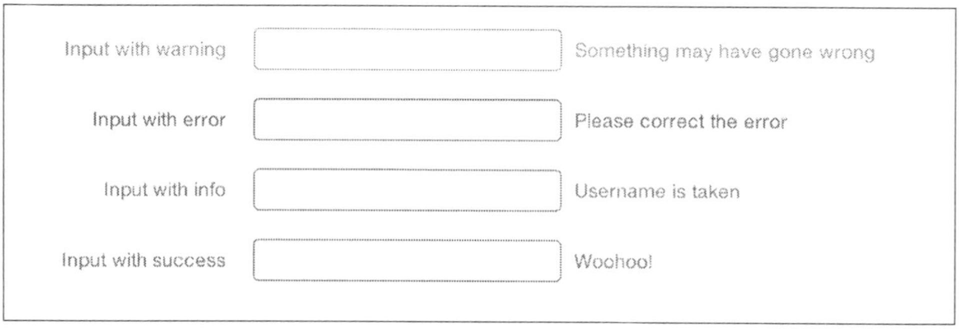

Figure 2-42. Validation states

Buttons

One of my favorite features of Bootstrap is the way that buttons are styled. Dave Winer, inventor of RSS and big fan of Bootstrap, has this to say about it:

> That this is needed, desperately needed, is indicated by the incredible uptake of Bootstrap. I use it in all the server software I'm working on. And it shows through in the templating language I'm developing, so everyone who uses it will find it's "just there" and works, any time you want to do a Bootstrap technique. Nothing to do, no libraries to include. It's as if it were part of the hardware. Same approach that Apple took with the Mac OS in 1984.
>
> — Dave Winer
> *scripting.com*

I like to think that Bootstrap is unifying the Web and allowing a unified experience of what an interface can look like across the Web. With the advent of Bootstrap, you can usually spot the sites that have adopted it by the buttons that they use. A grid layout and many of the other features fade into the background, but buttons, forms, and other unifying elements are a key part of Bootstrap. When I come across a site that is using Bootstrap, I want to give a high five to the webmaster at that domain, since he probably "just gets it." I felt the same way a few years ago whenever I saw wp-content in the HTML of sites that I visited.

Now, buttons and links can all look alike with Bootstrap. Anything that is given a class of `.btn` will inherit the default look of a gray button with rounded corners. However, you can add color to the buttons by adding extra classes (see Table 2-3).

Table 2-3. Button color examples

Buttons	Class	Description
Default	btn	Standard gray button with gradient
Primary	btn btn-primary	Provides extra visual weight and identifies the primary action in a set of buttons (blue)
Info	btn btn-info	Used as an alternative to the default styles (light blue)
Success	btn-success	Indicates a successful or positive action (green)
Warning	btn btn-warning	Indicates caution should be taken with this action (orange)
Danger	btn btn-danger	Indicates a dangerous or potentially negative action (red)
Inverse	btn btn-inverse	Alternate dark-gray button, not tied to a semantic action or use
Link	btn btn-link	De-emphasizes a button by making it look like a link while maintaining button behavior

There are issues with buttons not appearing in Internet Explorer 9 because it doesn't crop background gradients on rounded corners. Also, Internet Explorer doesn't work well with disabled button elements. The rendered text is gray with a nasty text shadow that hasn't been fixed.

Button Sizes

If you need larger or smaller buttons, simply add `.btn-large`, `.btn-small`, or `.btn-mini` to links or buttons (see Figure 2-43):

```
<p>
  <button class="btn btn-large btn-primary" type="button">Large button</button>
  <button class="btn btn-large" type="button">Large button</button>
</p>
<p>
  <button class="btn btn-primary" type="button">Default button</button>
  <button class="btn" type="button">Default button</button>
</p>
<p>
  <button class="btn btn-small btn-primary" type="button">Small button</button>
```

```
  <button class="btn btn-small" type="button">Small button</button>
</p>
<p>
  <button class="btn btn-mini btn-primary" type="button">Mini button</button>
  <button class="btn btn-mini" type="button">Mini button</button>
</p>
```

Figure 2-43. Different button sizes

If you want to create buttons that display like a block-level element, simply add the .btn-block class (see Figure 2-44). These buttons will display at 100% width:

```
<button class="btn btn-large btn-block btn-primary" type="button">Block-
level button</button>
<button class="btn btn-large btn-block" type="button">Block-level button</button>
```

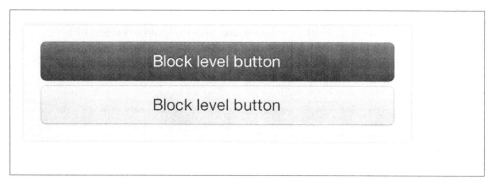

Figure 2-44. Block-level button

Disabled Button Styling

For anchor elements, simply add the class of .disabled to the tag and the link will fade in color, and lose the gradient (see Figure 2-45):

```
<a href="#" class="btn btn-large btn-primary disabled">Primary link</a>
<a href="#" class="btn btn-large disabled">Link</a>
```

Figure 2-45. Disabled link

 The .disabled class is being used much like the .active class. So, there's no .btn prefix, and remember, this is only for looks. You will need to use some JavaScript to actually disable the link.

For a button, simply add the disabled attribute to the button (see Figure 2-46). This will actually disable the button, so JavaScript is not directly needed:

```
<button type="button" class="btn btn-large btn-primary disabled"
disabled="disabled">Primary button</button>
<button type="button" class="btn btn-large" disabled>Button</button>
```

Figure 2-46. Disabled button

Images

Images have three classes (see Figure 2-47) that can be used to apply some simple styles: .img-rounded adds border-radius:6px to give the image rounded corners, .img-circle makes the entire image round by adding border-radius: 500px, and .img-polaroid adds a bit of padding and a gray border:

```
<img src="..." class="img-rounded">
<img src="..." class="img-circle">
<img src="..." class="img-polaroid">
```

Figure 2-47. Images

Icons

Bootstrap bundles 140 icons into one sprite that can be used with buttons, links, navigation, and form fields. The icons are provided by GLYPHICONS (*http://glyphicons.com/*); see Figure 2-48.

icon-glass	icon-music	icon-search	icon-envelope
icon-heart	icon-star	icon-star-empty	icon-user
icon-film	icon-th-large	icon-th	icon-th-list
icon-ok	icon-remove	icon-zoom-in	icon-zoom-out
icon-off	icon-signal	icon-cog	icon-trash
icon-home	icon-file	icon-time	icon-road
icon-download-alt	icon-download	icon-upload	icon-inbox
icon-play-circle	icon-repeat	icon-refresh	icon-list-alt
icon-lock	icon-flag	icon-headphones	icon-volume-off
icon-volume-down	icon-volume-up	icon-qrcode	icon-barcode
icon-tag	icon-tags	icon-book	icon-bookmark
icon-print	icon-camera	icon-font	icon-bold
icon-italic	icon-text-height	icon-text-width	icon-align-left
icon-align-center	icon-align-right	icon-align-justify	icon-list
icon-indent-left	icon-indent-right	icon-facetime-video	icon-picture
icon-pencil	icon-map-marker	icon-adjust	icon-tint
icon-edit	icon-share	icon-check	icon-move
icon-step-backward	icon-fast-backward	icon-backward	icon-play
icon-pause	icon-stop	icon-forward	icon-fast-forward
icon-step-forward	icon-eject	icon-chevron-left	icon-chevron-right
icon-plus-sign	icon-minus-sign	icon-remove-sign	icon-ok-sign
icon-question-sign	icon-info-sign	icon-screenshot	icon-remove-circle
icon-ok-circle	icon-ban-circle	icon-arrow-left	icon-arrow-right
icon-arrow-up	icon-arrow-down	icon-share-alt	icon-resize-full
icon-resize-small	icon-plus	icon-minus	icon-asterisk
icon-exclamation-sign	icon-gift	icon-leaf	icon-fire
icon-eye-open	icon-eye-close	icon-warning-sign	icon-plane
icon-calendar	icon-random	icon-comment	icon-magnet
icon-chevron-up	icon-chevron-down	icon-retweet	icon-shopping-cart
icon-folder-close	icon-folder-open	icon-resize-vertical	icon-resize-horizontal
icon-hdd	icon-bullhorn	icon-bell	icon-certificate
icon-thumbs-up	icon-thumbs-down	icon-hand-right	icon-hand-left
icon-hand-up	icon-hand-down	icon-circle-arrow-right	icon-circle-arrow-left
icon-circle-arrow-up	icon-circle-arrow-down	icon-globe	icon-wrench
icon-tasks	icon-filter	icon-briefcase	icon-fullscreen

Figure 2-48. Icons by GLYPHICONS

GLYPHICONS Attribution

Users of Bootstrap are fortunate to use the GLYPHICONS for free on Bootstrap projects. The developers have asked that you link back to GLYPHICONS when practical.

> GLYPHICONS Halflings are normally not available for free, but an arrangement between Bootstrap and the GLYPHICONS creators have made this possible at no cost to you as developers. As a thank you, we ask you to include an optional link back to GLYPHICONS whenever practical.
>
> — Bootstrap Documentation
> *http://getbootstrap.com*

Usage

To use the icons, simply use an `<i>` tag with the namespaced `.icon-` class. For example, if you want to use the edit icon, you add the `.icon-edit` class to the `<i>` tag:

```
<i class="icon-edit"></i>
```

If you want to use the white icon, simply add the `.icon-white` class to the tag:

```
<i class="icon-edit icon-white"></i>
```

Button groups

By using button groups combined with icons, you can create nice interface elements with minimal markup (see Figure 2-49):

```
<div class="btn-toolbar">
  <div class="btn-group">
    <a class="btn" href="#"><i class="icon-align-left"></i></a>
    <a class="btn" href="#"><i class="icon-align-center"></i></a>
    <a class="btn" href="#"><i class="icon-align-right"></i></a>
    <a class="btn" href="#"><i class="icon-align-justify"></i></a>
  </div>
</div>
```

Figure 2-49. Button groups

Navigation

When you are using icons next to a string of text, make sure to add a space to provide the proper alignment of the image (see Figure 2-50). Navigation code will be covered further in the next chapter.

```
<ul class="nav nav-list">
  <li class="active"><a href="#"><i class="icon-home icon-white"></i>
  Home</a></li>
  <li><a href="#"><i class="icon-book"></i> Library</a></li>
  <li><a href="#"><i class="icon-pencil"></i> Applications</a></li>
  <li><a href="#"><i class="i"></i> Misc</a></li>
</ul>
```

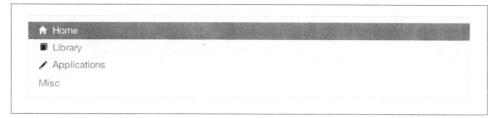

Figure 2-50. Basic navigation list

CHAPTER 3

Bootstrap Layout Components

In addition to all of the markup provided in the previous chapter, Bootstrap provides a toolkit of flexible components that can be used in designing application interfaces, web features, and more. All of the plugins are available in one separate JavaScript file, or you can use the Bootstrap customizer to pick and choose which plugins you want. Personally, on the projects that I build, I lump them all together. That way I have options.

Dropdown Menus

Dropdown menus are toggleable, contextual menus for displaying links in a list format. The dropdowns can be used on a variety of different elements, navs, buttons, and more. You can have a single dropdown or extend the dropdown into another submenu. You can see a basic dropdown menu in Figure 3-1.

Figure 3-1. Basic dropdown menu

The following code creates a basic dropdown menu:

```
<ul class="dropdown-menu" role="menu" aria-labelledby="dropdownMenu">
  <li><a tabindex="-1" href="#">Action</a></li>
  <li><a tabindex="-1" href="#">Another action</a></li>
  <li><a tabindex="-1" href="#">Something else here</a></li>
  <li class="divider"></li>
```

```
  <li><a tabindex="-1" href="#">Separated link</a></li>
</ul>
```

Options

Right-align

Add `.pull-right` to a `.dropdown-menu` to right-align the dropdown menu to the parent object:

```
<ul class="dropdown-menu pull-right" role="menu" aria-labelledby="dLabel">
  ...
</ul>
```

Submenu

If you would like to add a second layer of dropdowns (see Figure 3-2), simply add `.dropdown-submenu` to any `<li>` in an existing dropdown menu for automatic styling:

```
<ul class="dropdown-menu" role="menu" aria-labelledby="dLabel">
  ...
  <li class="dropdown-submenu">
    <a tabindex="-1" href="#">More options</a>
    <ul class="dropdown-menu">
      ...
    </ul>
  </li>
</ul>
```

Figure 3-2. Dropdown menu and submenu

Button Groups

Button groups allow multiple buttons to be stacked together (see Figure 3-3). This is useful when you want to place items like alignment buttons together. To create a button group, simply wrap a series of anchors or buttons in a `<div>` that has `.btn-group` as a class:

```
<div class="btn-group">
  <button class="btn">1</button>
  <button class="btn">2</button>
  <button class="btn">3</button>
</div>
```

Figure 3-3. Left, middle, and right button group

If you have multiple button groups (see Figure 3-4) that you want to place on a single line, wrap multiple `.btn-group` classes with `.btn-toolbar`:

```
<div class="btn-toolbar">
  <div class="btn-group">
    <a class="btn" href="#"><i class="icon-align-left"></i></a>
    <a class="btn" href="#"><i class="icon-align-center"></i></a>
    <a class="btn" href="#"><i class="icon-align-right"></i></a>
    <a class="btn" href="#"><i class="icon-align-justify"></i></a>
  </div>
  <div class="btn-group">
    <a class="btn" href="#"><i class="icon-italic"></i></a>
    <a class="btn" href="#"><i class="icon-bold"></i></a>
    <a class="btn" href="#"><i class="icon-font"></i></a>
    <a class="btn" href="#"><i class="icon-text-height"></i></a>
    <a class="btn" href="#"><i class="icon-text-width"></i></a>
  </div>
  <div class="btn-group">
    <a class="btn" href="#"><i class="icon-indent-left"></i></a>
    <a class="btn" href="#"><i class="icon-indent-right"></i></a>
  </div>
</div>
```

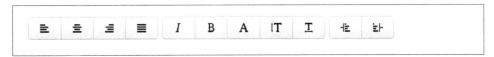

Figure 3-4. Button toolbar

For more information about using icons with buttons, follow the examples in Chapter 2.

To stack the buttons vertically (see Figure 3-5), add `.btn-group-vertical` to the `.btn-group` class:

```
<div class="btn-group btn-group-vertical">
  ...
</div>
```

Figure 3-5. Vertical button group

Button Groups as Radio Buttons and Checkboxes

To have the checkboxes function as radio buttons, where only one option can be selected at a time, or checkboxes, where multiple options can be selected, you simply need to add some extra markup and then Bootstrap's JavaScript will provide the rest. This will be covered in detail in Chapter 4.

 To use a button with a dropdown, it must be individually wrapped in its own .btn-group within a btn-toolbar for proper rendering.

Buttons with Dropdowns

To add a dropdown to a button (see Figure 3-6), simply wrap the button and dropdown menu in a .btn-group. You can also use <span class="caret"></span> to act as an indicator that the button is a dropdown:

```
<div class="btn-group">
  <button class="btn btn-danger">Danger</button>
  <button class="btn btn-danger dropdown-toggle" data-toggle="dropdown">
    <span class="caret"></span>
  </button>
  <ul class="dropdown-menu">
    <li><a href="#">Action</a></li>
    <li><a href="#">Another action</a></li>
    <li><a href="#">Something else here</a></li>
    <li class="divider"></li>
    <li><a href="#">Separated link</a></li>
  </ul>
</div>
```

Figure 3-6. Button with a dropdown

You can use the dropdowns with any button size: `.btn-large`, `.btn`, `.btn-small`, or `.btn-mini`. Figure 3-7 shows several examples of different button sizes.

Figure 3-7. Button dropdown sizes

Split Button Dropdowns

Split button dropdowns (see Figure 3-8) use the same general style as the dropdown button but add a primary action along with the dropdown. Split buttons have the primary action on the left and a toggle on the right that displays the dropdown.

Figure 3-8. Split button dropdown

Here's the code for a split button dropdown:

```
<div class="btn-group">
  <button class="btn">Action</button>
  <button class="btn dropdown-toggle" data-toggle="dropdown">
```

```
        <span class="caret"></span>
      </button>
      <ul class="dropdown-menu">
        <!-- dropdown menu links -->
      </ul>
    </div>
```

Dropup Menus

Menus can also be built to drop up rather than down (see Figure 3-9). To make this change, simply add `.dropup` to the `.btn-group` container. To have the button pull up from the righthand side, add `.pull-right` to the `.dropdown-menu` (take note: the caret is now pointed up because the menu will be going up instead of down):

```
<div class="btn-group dropup">
  <button class="btn">Dropup</button>
  <button class="btn dropdown-toggle" data-toggle="dropdown">
    <span class="caret"></span>
  </button>
  <ul class="dropdown-menu">
    <!-- dropdown menu links -->
  </ul>
</div>
```

Figure 3-9. Dropup menu

Navigation Elements

Bootstrap provides a few different options for styling navigation elements. All of them share the same markup and base class, `.nav`.

Bootstrap also provides a helper class, `.active`. In principle, it generally adds distinction to the current element and sets it apart from the rest of the navigation elements. You can add this class to the home page links or to the links of the page that the user is currently on.

Tabular Navigation

To create a tabbed navigation menu (see Figure 3-10), start with a basic unordered list
with the base class of .nav and add .nav-tabs:

```
<ul class="nav nav-tabs">
  <li class="active">
    <a href="#">Home</a>
  </li>
  <li><a href="#">Profile</a></li>
  <li><a href="#">Messages</a></li>
</ul>
```

Figure 3-10. Tabbed navigation

Basic Pills Navigation

To turn the tabs into pills (see Figure 3-11), use .nav-pills instead of .nav-tabs:

```
<ul class="nav nav-pills">
  <li class="active">
    <a href="#">Home</a>
  </li>
  <li><a href="#">Profile</a></li>
  <li><a href="#">Messages</a></li>
</ul>
```

Figure 3-11. Tabbed navigation

Disabled class

For each of the .nav classes, if you add the .disabled class, it will create a gray link that
also disables the :hover state (see Figure 3-12):

```
<ul class="nav nav-pills">
  ...
  <li class="disabled"><a href="#">Home</a></li>
  ...
</ul>
```

Clickable link   Clickable link   Disabled link

Figure 3-12. Disabled navigation

The link is still clickable unless the `href` is removed with JavaScript or some other method.

Stackable Navigation

Both tabs and pills are horizontal by default. To make them appear vertically stacked, just add the `.nav-stacked` class. See Figures 3-13 and 3-14 for examples of verticaly stacked tabs and pills.

Here's the code for stacked tabs:

```
<ul class="nav nav-tabs nav-stacked">
  ...
</ul>
```

Figure 3-13. Stacked tabs

Here's the code for stacked pills:

```
<ul class="nav nav-pills nav-stacked">
  ...
</ul>
```

Figure 3-14. Stacked pills

Dropdowns

Navigation menus share a similar syntax with dropdown menus (see Figure 3-15). By default, you have a list item that has an anchor working in conjunction with some data-attributes to trigger an unordered list with a `.dropdown-menu` class:

```
<ul class="nav nav-tabs">
    <li class="dropdown">
        <a class="dropdown-toggle"
            data-toggle="dropdown"
            href="#">
            Dropdown
            <b class="caret"></b>
        </a>
        <ul class="dropdown-menu">
    <li><a href="#">Action</a></li>
    <li><a href="#">Another action</a></li>
    <li><a href="#">Something else here</a></li>
    <li class="divider"></li>
    <li><a href="#">Separated link</a></li>
</ul>
    </li>
</ul>
```

Figure 3-15. Tabbed navigation with a dropdown menu

To do the same thing with pills (Figure 3-16), simply swap the `.nav-tabs` class with `.nav-pills`:

```
<ul class="nav nav-pills">
    <li class="dropdown">
        <a class="dropdown-toggle" data-toggle="dropdown" href="#">
            Dropdown
            <b class="caret"></b>
        </a>
        <ul class="dropdown-menu">
            <!--links-->
        </ul>
    </li>
</ul>
```

Figure 3-16. Pill navigation with dropdowns

Navigation Lists

Navigation lists are useful when you need to display a group of navigation links. This type of element is common when building admin interfaces. In the MAKE admin interface, for example, I have one of these on the sidebar of every page with quick links to common pages (see Figure 3-17). Bootstrap developers use a form of this for their documentation. Like all of the lists that we have discussed thus far, navigation lists are unordered lists with the `.nav` class. To give it its specific styling, we add the `.nav-list` class:

```
<ul class="nav nav-list">
        <li class="nav-header">List Header</li>
        <li class="active"><a href="/">Home</a></li>
        <li><a href="#">Library</a></li>
  <li><a href="#">Applications</a></li>
  <li class="nav-header">Another List Header</li>
  <li><a href="#">Profile</a></li>
        <li><a href="#">Settings</a></li>
  <li class="divider"></li>
  <li><a href="#">Help</a></li>
</ul>
```

Horizontal divider

To create a divider, much like an `<hr />`, use an empty `<li>` with a class of `.divider`:

```
<ul class="nav-menu">
    ...
        <li class="divider"></li>
        ....
</ul>
```

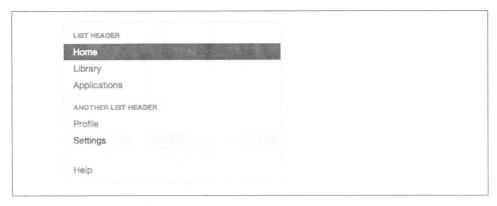

Figure 3-17. Navigation list

Tabbable Navigation

Not only can you create a tabbed navigation, but by using the JavaScript plugin, you can also add interaction by opening different windows of content (see Figure 3-18). To make navigation tabs, create a `.tab-pane` with a unique ID for every tab, and then wrap them in `.tab-content`:

```
<div class="tabbable">
      <ul class="nav nav-tabs">
         <li class="active"><a href="#tab1" data-toggle="tab">Meats</a></li>
         <li><a href="#tab2" data-toggle="tab">More Meat</a></li>
      </ul>
      <div class="tab-content">
         <div class="tab-pane active" id="tab1">
               <p>Bacon ipsum dolor sit amet jerky flank...</p>
         </div>
         <div class="tab-pane" id="tab2">
               <p>Beef ribs, turducken ham hock...</p>
         </div>
      </div>
</div>
```

Meats	More Meat

Bacon ipsum dolor sit amet jerky flank andouille, ham hock spare ribs pork loin jowl meatloaf boudin. Beef ribs brisket boudin beef bacon. Beef ribs shoulder ball tip capicola rump. Sausa bone flank ball tip short ribs andouille ground round. Ham hock turducken beef ribs prosciutto chicken. Pig chuck meatloaf, strip steak ribeye doner fatback chicken shankle ball tip pancet

Figure 3-18. Tabbable navigation example

If you want to make the tabs fade when switching, add `.fade` to each `.tab-pane`.

Tab position

The tabs are fully positionable; you can have them above, below, or on the sides of the content (see Figure 3-19).

Figure 3-19. Bottom tabs

Here's the code for positioning tabs:

```
<div class="tabbable tabs-below">
  <div class="tab-content">
    <div class="tab-pane active" id="tab1">
      <p>I'm in Section A.</p>
    </div>
    <div class="tab-pane" id="tab2">
      <p>I'm in Section B.</p>
    </div>
    <div class="tab-pane" id="tab3">
      <p>I'm in Section C.</p>
    </div>
  </div>
  <ul class="nav nav-tabs">
    <li class="active"><a href="#tab1" data-toggle="tab">Section A</a></li>
    <li><a href="#tab2" data-toggle="tab">Section B</a></li>
    <li><a href="#tab3" data-toggle="tab">Section C</a></li>
  </ul>
</div>
```

Tabs on the left (see Figure 3-20) get the `.tabs-left` class. For this, you need to swap the tab content and the tabs:

```
<div class="tabbable tabs-left">
  <ul class="nav nav-tabs">
    <li class="active"><a href="#tab1" data-toggle="tab">Section A</a></li>
    <li><a href="#tab2" data-toggle="tab">Section B</a></li>
    <li><a href="#tab3" data-toggle="tab">Section C</a></li>
  </ul>
  <div class="tab-content">
    <div class="tab-pane active" id="tab1">
      <p>I'm in Section A.</p>
    </div>
    <div class="tab-pane" id="tab2">
      <p>I'm in Section B.</p>
```

```
      </div>
      <div class="tab-pane" id="tab3">
        <p>I'm in Section C.</p>
      </div>
    </div>
  </div>
</div>
```

Figure 3-20. Left tabs

Tabs on the right get the .tabs-right class (see Figure 3-21):

```
<div class="tabbable tabs-right">
  <ul class="nav nav-tabs">
    <li class="active"><a href="#tab1" data-toggle="tab">Section A</a></li>
    <li><a href="#tab2" data-toggle="tab">Section B</a></li>
    <li><a href="#tab3" data-toggle="tab">Section C</a></li>
  </ul>
  <div class="tab-content">
    <div class="tab-pane active" id="tab1">
      <p>I'm in section A.</p>
    </div>
    <div class="tab-pane" id="tab2">
      <p>I'm in section B.</p>
    </div>
    <div class="tab-pane" id="tab3">
      <p>I'm in section C.</p>
    </div>
  </div>
</div>
```

Figure 3-21. Right tabs

As a footnote to the tabbable elements, you can use the markup here to control a variety of things that are perhaps outside of the scope of the default usage mechanism. On MAKE's site, I use this to control the navigation and subnavigation. When you click on the navigation menu, the subnavigation changes and shows different links.

Navbar

The navbar is a nice feature, and is one of the prominent features of Bootstrap sites (see Figure 3-22). At its core, the navbar includes styling for site names and basic navigation. It can later be extended by adding form-specific controls and specialized dropdowns. To be sure that the navbar is constrained to the width of the content of the page, either place it inside of a `.span12` or the `.container` class:

```
<div class="navbar">
  <div class="navbar-inner">
    <a class="brand" href="#">Title</a>
    <ul class="nav">
      <li class="active"><a href="#">Home</a></li>
      <li><a href="#">Link</a></li>
      <li><a href="#">Link</a></li>
    </ul>
  </div>
</div>
```

Figure 3-22. Basic navbar

Note the `.brand` class in the code. This will give the text a lighter `font-weight` and slightly larger size.

```
<a class="brand" href="#">Project name</a>
```

Navbar Links

To add links to the navbar (see Figure 3-23), simply add an unordered list with a class of `.nav`. If you want to add a divider to your links, you can do that by adding an empty list item with a class of `.divider-vertical`:

```
<ul class="nav">
  <li class="active"><a href="#">Home</a></li>
  <li><a href="#">First Link</a></li>
  <li><a href="#">Second Link</a></li>
```

```
<li class="divider-vertical"></li>
<li><a href="#">Third Link</a></li>
</ul>
```

Figure 3-23. Nav links

Forms

Instead of using the default class-based forms from Chapter 2, forms that are in the navbar use the `.navbar-form` class. This ensures that the form's margins are properly set and match the nav stylings (see Figure 3-24). Of note, `.pull-left` and `.pull-right` helper classes may help move the form into the proper position:

```
<form class="navbar-form pull-left">
        <input type="text" class="span2" id="fname">
        <button type="submit" class="btn">
</form>
```

Figure 3-24. Default navbar form

To add rounded corners (see Figure 3-25), as seen in the search inputs of iOS devices, use the `.navbar-search` class instead of the `.navbar-form`:

```
<form class="navbar-search"  accept-charset="utf-8">
        <input type="text" class="search-query" placeholder="Search">
</form>
```

Figure 3-25. Navbar search input

Navbar Menu Variations

The Bootstrap navbar can be dynamic in its positioning. By default, it is a block-level element that takes its positioning based on its placement in the HTML. With a few helper classes, you can place it either on the top or bottom of the page, or you can make it scroll statically with the page.

Fixed top navbar

If you want the navbar fixed to the top, add `.navbar-fixed-top` to the `.navbar` class. To prevent the navbar from sitting on top of other content in the body of the page, add at least 40 pixels of padding to the <body> tag:

```
<div class="navbar navbar-fixed-top">
  <div class="navbar-inner">
    <a class="brand" href="#">Title</a>
    <ul class="nav">
      <li class="active"><a href="#">Home</a></li>
      <li><a href="#">Link</a></li>
      <li><a href="#">Link</a></li>
    </ul>
  </div>
</div>
```

Fixed bottom navbar

To affix the navbar to the bottom of the page, simply add the `.fixed-navbar-bottom` class to the navbar. Once again, to prevent overlap, add at least 40 pixels of padding to the <body> tag:

```
<div class="navbar navbar-fixed-bottom">
 <div class="navbar-inner">
    <a class="brand" href="#">Title</a>
    <ul class="nav">
      <li class="active"><a href="#">Home</a></li>
      <li><a href="#">Link</a></li>
      <li><a href="#">Link</a></li>
    </ul>
  </div>
</div>
```

Static top navbar

To create a navbar that scrolls with the page, add the `.navbar-static-top` class. This class does not require adding the padding to the <body>:

```
<div class="navbar navbar-static-top">
  <div class="navbar-inner">
    <a class="brand" href="#">Title</a>
    <ul class="nav">
      <li class="active"><a href="#">Home</a></li>
      <li><a href="#">Link</a></li>
      <li><a href="#">Link</a></li>
    </ul>
```

```
      </div>
    </div>
```

Responsive navbar

Like the rest of Bootstrap, the navbar can be totally responsive as shown in
Figure 3-26. To add the responsive features, the content that you want to be collapsed
needs to be wrapped in a <div> with .nav-collapse.collapse as a class. The collapsing
nature is tripped by a button that has a the class of .btn-navbar and then features two
data- elements. The first, data-toggle, is used to tell the JavaScript what to do with
the button, and the second, data-target, indicates which element to toggle. Three
<spans> with a class of .icon-bar create what I like to call the hamburger button. This
will toggle the elements that are in the .nav-collapse <div>. For this feature to work,
the *bootstrap-responsive.css* and either the *collapse.js* or the full *bootstrap.js* files must
be included.

Figure 3-26. Responsive navbar

Use the following code to create a responsive navbar:

```
<div class="header">
  <div class="navbar-inner">
    <div class="container">
      <a class="btn btn-navbar" data-toggle="collapse"
      data-target=".nav-collapse">
        <span class="icon-bar"></span>
        <span class="icon-bar"></span>
        <span class="icon-bar"></span>
      </a>
```

```
<!-- Leave the brand out if you want it to be shown when other elements
are collapsed... -->
<a href="#" class="brand">Project Name</a>

<!-- Everything that you want collapsed, should be added to the collapse
div. -->
<div class="nav-collapse collapse">
  <!-- .nav, .navbar-search etc... -->
</div>

    </div>
  </div>
</div>
```

Inverted navbar

To create an inverted navbar with a black background and white text as shown in Figure 3-27, simply add `.navbar-inverse` to the `.navbar` class:

```
<div class="navbar navbar-inverse">
      ...
</div>
```

Figure 3-27. Inverted navbar

Breadcrumbs

Breadcrumbs are a great way to show hierarchy-based information for a site (see Figure 3-28). In the case of blogs, breadcrumbs can show the dates of publishing, categories, or tags. A breadcrumb in Bootstrap is simply an unordered list with a class of `.breadcrumb`. There is a also a helper class of `.divider` that mutes the colors and makes the text a little smaller. You can use forward slashes, arrows, or any divided that you choose. Note that the divider in the breadcrumbs has a slightly different markup than the navbar example.

The following code uses the class `.breadcrumb`:

```
<ul class="breadcrumb">
    <li><a href="#">Home</a> <span class="divider">/</span></li>
        <li><a href="#">2012</a> <span class="divider">/</span></li>
        <li><a href="#">December</a> <span class="divider">/</span></li>
        <li><a href="#">5</a></li>
</ul>
```

```
<ul class="breadcrumb">
  <li><a href="#">Home</a> <span class="divider">&rarr;</span></li>
  <li><a href="#">Dinner Menu</a> <span class="divider">&rarr;</span></li>
  <li><a href="#">Specials</a> <span class="divider">&rarr;</span></li>
  <li><a href="#">Steaks</a></li>
</ul>

<ul class="breadcrumb">
  <li><a href="#">Home</a> <span class="divider">&raquo;</span></li>
  <li><a href="#">Electronics</a> <span class="divider">&raquo;</span></li>
  <li><a href="#">Raspberry Pi</a></li>
</ul>
```

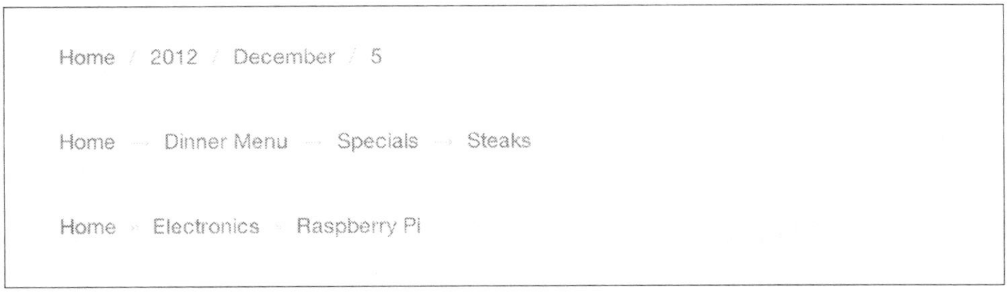

Figure 3-28. Breadcrumb

Pagination

Bootstrap handles pagination like a lot of other interface elements, an unordered list, with wrapper a `<div>` that has a specific class that identifies the element. In the basic form, adding `.pagination` to the parent `<div>` creates a row of bordered links. Each of the list items can be additionally styled by using the `.disabled` or `.active` class. See Figures 3-29 and 3-30 for examples of this.

Here's the code for basic pagination:

```
<div class="pagination">
  <ul>
    <li><a href="#">&laquo;</a></li>
    <li><a href="#">1</a></li>
    <li><a href="#">2</a></li>
    <li><a href="#">3</a></li>
    <li><a href="#">4</a></li>
    <li><a href="#">5</a></li>
    <li><a href="#">&raquo;</a></li>
  </ul>
</div>
```

Figure 3-29. Basic pagination

And here's the code for pagination using helper classes:

```
<div class="pagination pagination-centered">
  <ul>
    <li class="disabled"><a href="#">«</a></li>
    <li class="active"><a href="#">1</a></li>
    <li><a href="#">2</a></li>
    <li><a href="#">3</a></li>
    <li><a href="#">4</a></li>
    <li><a href="#">5</a></li>
    <li><a href="#">»</a></li>
  </ul>
</div>
```

« 1 2 3 4 5 »

Figure 3-30. Pagination with helper classes

In addition to the `.active` and `.disabled` classes for list items, you can add `.pagination-centered` to the parent `<div>`. This will center the contents of the `<div>`. If you want the items right-aligned in the `<div>`, add `.pagination-right`. For sizing, in addition to the normal size, there are three other sizes that can be applied by adding a class to the wrapper `<div>`: `.pagination-large`, `.pagination-small`, and `.pagination-mini` (see Figure 3-31):

```
<div class="pagination pagination-large">
  <ul>
    ...
  </ul>
</div>
<div class="pagination">
  <ul>
    ...
  </ul>
</div>
<div class="pagination pagination-small">
  <ul>
    ...
  </ul>
</div>
<div class="pagination pagination-mini">
```

```
<ul>
  ...
</ul>
</div>
```

Figure 3-31. Pagination sizes

Pager

If you need to create simple pagination links that go beyond text, the pager can work quite well. Like the pagination links, the markup is an unordered list that sheds the wrapper <div>. By default, the links are centered (see Figure 3-32).

Figure 3-32. Basic pager

The following is the code for a basic pager:

```
<ul class="pager">
  <li><a href="#">Previous</a></li>
  <li><a href="#">Next</a></li>
</ul>
```

To left- or right-align the links, you just need to add the .previous and .next class as to the list items (see Figure 3-33). Also, like .pagination in Figure 3-31, you can add the .disabled class for a muted look.

Figure 3-33. Aligned page links

The following is the code for aligning page links:

```
<ul class="pager">
  <li class="previous">
    <a href="#">&larr; Older</a>
  </li>
  <li class="next">
    <a href="#">Newer &rarr;</a>
  </li>
</ul>
```

Labels

Labels are great for offering counts, tips, or other markup for pages. They're another of my favorite little Bootstrap touches. Figure 3-34 shows some labels that can be used.

Figure 3-34. Labels

Here's the code to use these labels:

```
<span class="label">Default</span>
<span class="label label-success">Success</span>
<span class="label label-warning">Warning</span>
<span class="label label-important">Important</span>
<span class="label label-info">Info</span>
<span class="label label-inverse">Inverse</span>
```

Badges

Badges are similar to labels; the primary difference is that the corners are more rounded. The colors of badges reflect the same classes as labels (see Figure 3-35).

Figure 3-35. Badges

The following code shows how to use badges:

```
<span class="badge">1</span>
<span class="badge badge-success">2</span>
<span class="badge badge-warning">4</span>
<span class="badge badge-important">6</span>
```

```
<span class="badge badge-info">8</span>
<span class="badge badge-inverse">10</span>
```

Typographic Elements

In addition to buttons, labels, forms, tables, and tabs, Bootstrap has a few more elements for basic page layout.

Hero Unit

The hero unit is a large content area that increases the size of headings and adds a lot of margin for landing page content (see Figure 3-36). To use the hero unit, simply create a container `<div>` with the class of `.hero-unit`. In addition to a larger `<h1>`, the `font-weight` is reduced to 200 :

```
<div class="hero-unit">
  <h1>Hello, World!</h1>
  <p>This is a simple hero unit, a simple jumbotron-style component for calling
  extra attention to featured content or information.</p>
  <p><a class="btn btn-primary btn-large">Learn more</a></p>
</div>
```

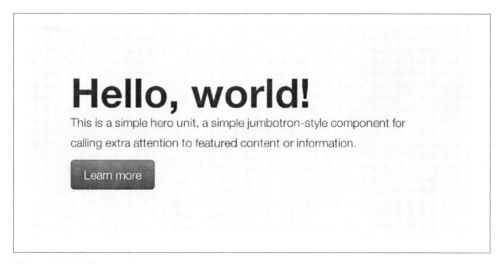

Figure 3-36. Hero unit

Page Header

The page header (see Figure 3-37) is a nice little feature to add appropriate spacing around the headings on a page. This is particularly helpful on a blog archive page where you may have several post titles and need a way to add distinction to each of them. To use a page header, wrap your heading in a `<div>` with a class of `.page-header`:

```
<div class="page-header">
  <h1>Example page header <small>Subtext for header</small></h1>
</div>
```

Example page header Subtext for header

Figure 3-37. Page header

Thumbnails

A lot of sites need a way to lay out images in a grid, and Bootstrap has an easy way to do this. To create a thumbnail, add an `<a>` tag with the class of `.thumbnail` around an image. This adds four pixels of padding and a gray border (see Figure 3-38). On hover, an animated glow outlines the image.

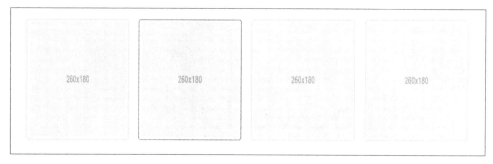

Figure 3-38. Basic thumbnail

Use the following code to create a thumbnail:

```
<a href="#" class="thumbnail">
  <img alt="Kittens!" style="" src="http://placekitten.com/300/250">
</a>
```

Now that you have your basic thumbnail, you can add headings, buttons, and more as shown in Figure 3-39; just change the `<a>` tag that has a class of `.thumbnail` to a `<div>`. Inside of that `<div>`, you can add anything you need. Since this is a `<div>`, we can use the default span-based naming convention for sizing. If you want to group multiple images, place them in an unordered list, and each list item will be floated to the left.

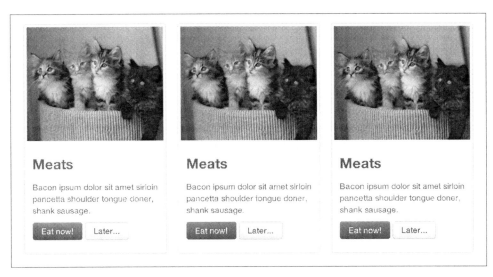

Figure 3-39. Extended thumbnail

The following code shows how to extend and add more to the thumbnail:

```
<ul class="thumbnails">
  <li class="span4">
    <div class="thumbnail">
      <img data-src="holder.js/300x200" alt="300x200" style="">
      <div class="caption">
        <h3>Meats</h3>
        <p>Bacon ipsum dolor sit amet sirloin pancetta shoulder tongue doner,
          shank sausage.</p>
        <p><a href="#" class="btn btn-primary">Eat now!</a> <a href="#"
          class="btn">Later...</a></p>
      </div>
    </div>
  </li>
  <li class="span4">
    ...
  </li>
</ul>
```

Alerts

Like the modals that will be described in Chapter 4, alerts provide a way to style messages to the user (see Figure 3-40). The default alert is added by creating a wrapper <div> and adding a class of .alert:

```
<div class="alert">
    <a href="#" class="close" data-dismiss="alert">&times;</a>
    <strong>Warning!</strong> Not to be alarmist, but you have now been alerted.
</div>
```

Figure 3-40. Basic alert

The .alert uses the alerts jQuery plugin that is discussed in Chapter 4. To close the alert, you can use a button that contains the data-dismiss="alert" attribute. Mobile Safari and Mobile Opera browsers require an href="#" to close.

If you have a longer message in your alert, you can use the .alert-block class. This provides a little more padding above and below the content contained in the alert, which is particularly useful for multi-page lines of content (see Figure 3-41).

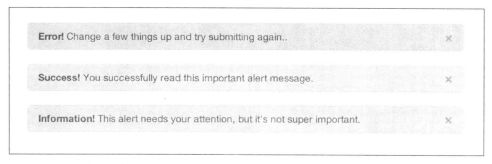

Figure 3-41. Alert block

There are also three other color options as shown in Figure 3-42 to help provide a more semantic method for the alert. They are added by using either .alert-error, .alert-success, or .alert-info.

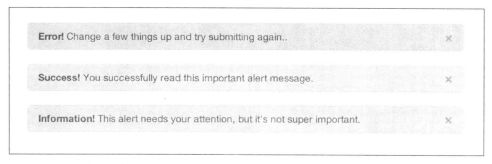

Figure 3-42. Alert color options

Progress Bars

The purpose of progress bars is to show that assets are loading, in progress, or that there is action taking place regarding elements on the page. Personally, I think that these elements are just an exercise in markup and have little purpose beyond that in the

Bootstrap framework. That being said, among the thousands of people using Bootstrap, there are likely a few outliers who have a good reason for building progress bars. By nature, these are static elements that need some sort of JavaScript method to provide any interaction.

The default progress bar has a light gray background and a blue progress bar as shown in Figure 3-43. To create it, add a <div> with a class of .progress. Inside, add an empty <div> with a class of .bar. Add a style attribute with the width expressed as a percentage. I added style="60%"; to indicate that the progress bar was at 60%:

```
<div class="progress">
  <div class="bar" style="width: 60%;"></div>
</div>
```

Figure 3-43. Default progress bar

To create a striped progress bar (see Figure 3-44),[1] just add .progress-striped to the container <div>:

```
<div class="progress progress-striped">
  <div class="bar" style="width: 20%;"></div>
</div>
```

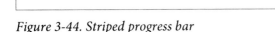

Figure 3-44. Striped progress bar

Like the striped version of the progress bar, you can animate the stripes (see Figure 3-45 for a static image of this), making it look like a blue light special barbershop pole.

Figure 3-45. Animated progress bar

Here's the code to animate the progress bar:

1. Striped progress bars are not available in Internet Explorer 7 and 8.

```
<div class="progress progress-striped active">
  <div class="bar" style="width: 40%;"></div>
</div>
```

In addition to the blue progress bar, there are options for green, yellow, and red using the `.bar-success`, `.bar-warning`, and `.bar-danger` classes. Progress bars can be stacked (see Figure 3-46), indicating a graph of sorts by adding multiple elements together using this code:

```
<div class="progress">
  <div class="bar bar-success" style="width: 35%;"></div>
  <div class="bar bar-warning" style="width: 20%;"></div>
  <div class="bar bar-danger" style="width: 10%;"></div>
</div>
```

Figure 3-46. Stacked progress bar

Media Object

When you look at social sites like Facebook, Twitter, and others, and strip away some of the formatting from timelines, you will see the media object (see Figure 3-47). Driven by the Bootstrap community and based on principles from the oocss community (*http://oocss.org/*), the goal of the media object is to make the code for developing these blocks of information drastically shorter. Nicole Sullivan-Hass shares a few elements of the media object similar to Bootstrap's on her site (*http://bit.ly/media-object-saves-post*). The media object is designed to literally save hundreds of lines of code, making it easy to customize.

Figure 3-47. Media object

Bootstrap leaves the design and formatting to you but provides a simple way to get going. Like a lot of other tools in Bootstrap, the goal of media objects (light markup, easy extendability) is achieved by applying classes to some simple markup. There are two forms to the media object: .media and .media-list. Figure 3-48 shows the former form. If you are preparing a list where the items will be part of an unordered list, use .media-list. If you are using only just <div> elements, use the .media object:

```
<div class="media">
  <a class="pull-left" href="#">
    <img class="media-object" data-src="holder.js/64x64">
  </a>
  <div class="media-body">
    <h4 class="media-heading">Media heading</h4>
    <p>...</p>

    <!-- Nested media object -->
    <div class="media">
      ...
    </div>
  </div>
</div>
```

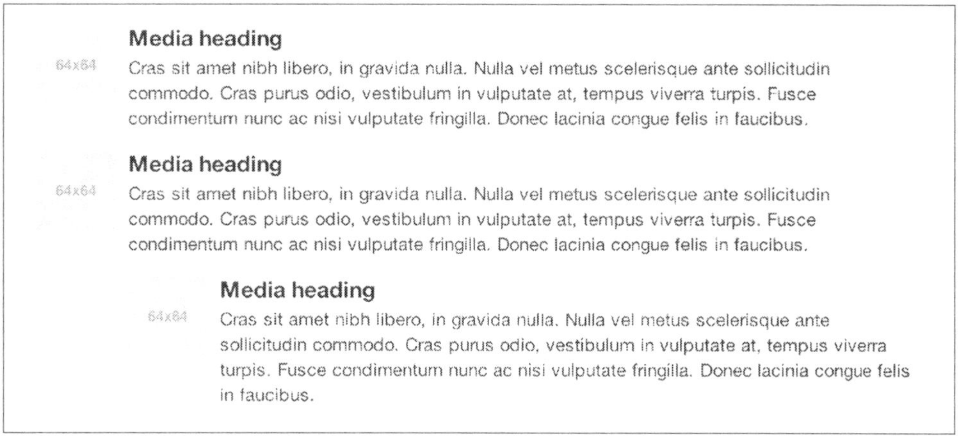

Media heading
64x64 Cras sit amet nibh libero, in gravida nulla. Nulla vel metus scelerisque ante sollicitudin commodo. Cras purus odio, vestibulum in vulputate at, tempus viverra turpis. Fusce condimentum nunc ac nisi vulputate fringilla. Donec lacinia congue felis in faucibus.

Media heading
64x64 Cras sit amet nibh libero, in gravida nulla. Nulla vel metus scelerisque ante sollicitudin commodo. Cras purus odio, vestibulum in vulputate at, tempus viverra turpis. Fusce condimentum nunc ac nisi vulputate fringilla. Donec lacinia congue felis in faucibus.

Media heading
64x64 Cras sit amet nibh libero, in gravida nulla. Nulla vel metus scelerisque ante sollicitudin commodo. Cras purus odio, vestibulum in vulputate at, tempus viverra turpis. Fusce condimentum nunc ac nisi vulputate fringilla. Donec lacinia congue felis in faucibus.

Figure 3-48. Default media object

To use media list (shown in Figure 3-49), change the container <div> to an <ul> and add the class .media-list. Since you can nest media objects, it is handy to markup for comments or other lists.

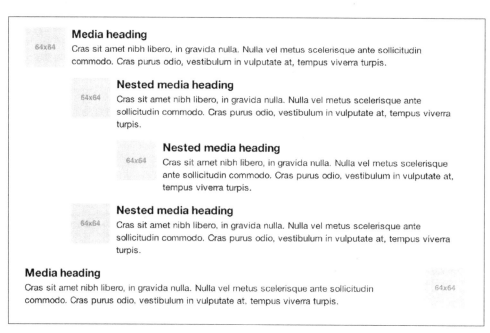

Figure 3-49. Media list example

The following code creates a media list:

```
<ul class="media-list">
  <li class="media">
    <a class="pull-left" href="#">
      <img class="media-object" data-src="holder.js/64x64">
    </a>
    <div class="media-body">
      <h4 class="media-heading">Media heading</h4>
      <p>...</p>
      ...

      <!-- Nested media object -->
      <div class="media">
        ...
      </div>
    </div>
  </li>
</ul>
```

Miscellaneous

There are a few more Bootstrap components that we have yet to cover in this chapter. Some of these components are layout-based, and a few are production-based helper classes. The first among these are the wells.

Wells

A well is a container `<div>` that causes the content to appear sunken on the page (see Figure 3-50). I have used wells for blog post meta information like author, date, and categories. To create a well, simply wrap the content that you would like to appear in the well with a `<div>` containing the class of `.well`:

```
<div class="well">
  ...
</div>
```

Look, I'm in a well!

Figure 3-50. Well

There are two additional classes that can be used in conjunction with `.well`: `.well-large` and `.well-small`. These affect the padding, making the well larger or smaller depending on the class (see Figure 3-51).

Look, I'm in a .well-large!

Look, I'm in a .well-small!

Figure 3-51. Well optional classes

The following code uses the well classes:

```
<div class="well well-large">

  Look, I'm in a .well-large!

</div>

<div class="well well-small">

  Look, I'm in a .well-small!

</div>
```

Helper Classes

Here are some helper classes that might come in handy.

Pull left

To float an element to the left, use the `.pull-left` class:

```
<div class="pull-left">
  ...
</div>

.pull-left {
  float: left;
}
```

Pull right

To float an element to the right, use the `.pull-right` class:

```
<div class="pull-right">
  ...
</div>

.pull-right {
  float: right;
}
```

Clearfix

To clear the float of any element, use the `.clearfix` class. When you have two elements of different sizes that are floated alongside each other, it is necessary to force the following elements in the the code below or to *clear* the preceding content. You can do this with a simple empty <div> with the class :of `.clearfix`:

```
<div class="clearfix"></div>

.clearfix {
  *zoom: 1;
  &:before,
  &:after {
    display: table;
    content: "";
  }
  &:after {
    clear: both;
  }
}
```

CHAPTER 4

Bootstrap JavaScript Plugins

The components discussed in Chapter 3 are just the beginning. Bootstrap comes bundled with 13 jQuery plugins that extend the features and can add more interaction to your site. To get started with Bootstrap's JavaScript plugins, you don't need to be an advanced JavaScript developer. In fact, by utilizing Bootstrap Data API, most of the plugins can be triggered without writing a single line of code.

Overview

Bootstrap can be included on your site in two forms, either compiled or raw. In Bootstrap 2.2.2, the uncompressed file is 59KB and the minimized version is only 32KB. All of the Bootstrap plugins are accessible using the included Data API. With this, you don't need to include a single line of JavaScript to invoke any of the plugin features.

Typically, JavaScript lies in a either a separate file or at the bottom of the page before the closing `</body>` tag. You can either use the `src` attribute to link to another file, or you can write the contents of the file between the opening and closing tags:

```
<!-- To reference another JavaScript file -->
<script src="assets/js/javaScript.js"></script>

<!-- To write JavaScript to the page -->
<script type="text/javaScript">
        function js_alert{
                alert('Page has loaded');
        }
</script>
```

Generally, it is best to include all JavaScript calls into a check that ensures that the DOM has been loaded on the page. If you have the JavaScript trying to fire earlier, it may miss elements as the browser parses the page. With jQuery, adding a check is easily done by selecting the document or the entire content of the page, and then applying the .ready() method:

```
$(document).ready(function(){
        alert('Page has loaded');
        // Once the page has loaded and is ready, an alert will fire.
});
```

As mentioned above, Bootstrap has a Data API where you can write data attributes into the HTML of the page. If you need to turn off the Data API, you can unbind the attributes by adding the following line of JavaScript:

```
$('body').off('.data-api')
```

If you need to disable a single plugin, you can do it programmatically using the namespace of the plugin along with the data-api namespace:

```
$('body').off('.alert.data-api')
```

Programmatic API

The developers of Bootstrap believe that you should be able to use all of the plugins throughout the JavaScript API. All public APIs are single, chainable methods and return the collection acted upon.

```
$('.btn.danger').button('toggle').addClass('active')
```

All methods should accept an optional options object, a string which targets a particular method, or nothing (which initiates a plugin with default behavior).

```
$("#myModal").modal()   // initialized with defaults
$("#myModal").modal({ keyboard: false })        // initialized with no keyboard
$("#myModal").modal('show')      // initializes and invokes show immediately
```

Transitions

The transition plugin provides simple transition effects. A few examples include:

- Sliding or fading in modals
- Fading out tabs
- Fading out alerts
- Sliding carousel panes

Modal

A modal is a child window that is layered over its parent window (see Figure 4-1). Typically, the purpose is to display content from a separate source that can have some interaction without leaving the parent window. Child windows can provide information, interaction, or more. I use them as a window for holding slideshows and login/registration information. The modal plugin is probably one of my favorite Bootstrap features.

To create a static modal window, use this code:

```
<div class="modal hide fade">
  <div class="modal-header">
    <button type="button" class="close" data-dismiss="modal" aria-hidden="true">
    &times;</button>
    <h3>Modal header</h3>
  </div>
  <div class="modal-body">
    <p>One fine body...</p>
  </div>
  <div class="modal-footer">
    <a href="#" class="btn">Close</a>
    <a href="#" class="btn btn-primary">Save changes</a>
  </div>
</div>
```

Figure 4-1. Static modal window

To invoke the modal window, you need to have some kind of a trigger. Normally I use a button or a link. If you look in the code below, you will see that in the `<a>` tag, the `href="myModal"` is the target of the modal that you want to load on the page. This code allows you to create multiple modals on the page and then have different triggers for each of them. Now, to be clear, you don't load multiple modals at the same time, but you can create many on the page to be loaded at different times.

There are three classes to take note of in the modal. The first is `.modal`, which is simply identifying the content of the `<div>` as a modal. The second is `.hide`, which tells the browser to hide the content of the `<div>` until we are ready to invoke it. And last, the `.fade` class. When the modal is toggled, it will cause the content to fade in and out.

```
<!-- Button to trigger modal -->
<a href="#myModal" role="button" class="btn" data-toggle="modal">Launch demo
modal</a>

<!-- Modal -->
<div id="myModal" class="modal hide fade" tabindex="-1" role="dialog"
aria-labelledby="myModalLabel" aria-hidden="true">
  <div class="modal-header">
    <button type="button" class="close" data-dismiss="modal"
    aria-hidden="true">×</button>
    <h3 id="myModalLabel">Modal header</h3>
  </div>
  <div class="modal-body">
    <p>One fine body…</p>
  </div>
  <div class="modal-footer">
    <button class="btn" data-dismiss="modal"
    aria-hidden="true">Close</button>
    <button class="btn btn-primary">Save changes</button>
  </div>
</div>
```

Usage

Using the Bootstrap JavaScript Data API, you simply need to pass a few data attributes to toggle the slideshow. To start with, set `data-toggle="modal"` on the link or button that you want to use to invoke the modal and then set the `data-target="#foo"` to the ID of the modal that you'd like to use.

To call a modal with `id="myModal"`, use a single line of JavaScript:

```
$('#myModal').modal(options)
```

Options

Options can either be passed in via data attributes or with JavaScript. To use the data attributes, prepend `data-` to the option name (e.g., `data-backdrop=""`). See Table 4-1 for descriptions of some modal options.

Table 4-1. Modal options

Name	Type	Default	Description
backdrop	Boolean	true	Set to false if you don't want the modal to be closed when the user clicks outside of the modal.
keyboard	Boolean	true	Closes the modal when escape key is pressed; set to false to disable.
show	Boolean	true	Shows the modal when initialized.
remote	path	false	Using the jQuery `.load` method, inject content into the modal body. If an `href` with a valid URL is added, it will load that content.

Methods

The following are some useful methods to use with modals.

Options

Activates your content as a modal. Accepts an optional options object.

`.modal(options)`.

```
$('#myModal').modal({
        keyboard: false
})
```

Toggle

Manually toggles a modal.

`.modal('toggle')`.

```
$('#myModal').modal('toggle')
```

Show

Manually opens a modal.

`.modal('show')`.

```
$('#myModal').modal('show')
```

Hide

Manually hides a modal.

`.modal('hide')`.

```
$('#myModal').modal('hide')
```

Events

Bootstrap provides the events listed in Table 4-2 if you need to hook into the function.

Table 4-2. Modal events

Event	Description
show	Fired after the show method is called.
shown	Fired when the modal has been made visible to the user.
hide	Fired when the hide instance method has been called.
hidden	Fired when the modal has finished being hidden from the user.

As an example, after the modal is hidden, you could cause an alert to fire:

```
$('#myModal').on('hidden', function () {
        alert('Hey girl, I heard you like modals...');
})
```

Dropdown

The dropdown was covered extensively in Chapter 3, but the interaction was glossed over. As a refresher, dropdowns can be added to the navbar, pills, tabs, and buttons.

Usage

To use a dropdown (Figure 4-2), add `data-toggle="dropdown"` to a link or button to toggle the dropdown.

Figure 4-2. Dropdown within navbar

Here's the code for developing a dropdown with data attributes:

```
<li class="dropdown">
  <a href="#" id="drop" role="button" class="dropdown-toggle"
  data-toggle="dropdown">Word <b class="caret"></b></a>
  <ul class="dropdown-menu" role="menu" aria-labelledby="drop">
    <li><a tabindex="-1" href="#">MAKE magazine</a></li>
    <li><a tabindex="-1" href="#">WordPress DevelopmentS</a></li>
    <li><a tabindex="-1" href="#">Speaking Engagements</a></li>
    <li class="divider"></li>
    <li><a tabindex="-1" href="#">Social Media</a></li>
  </ul>
</li>
```

If you need to keep links intact (which is useful if the browser is not enabling JavaScript), use the `data-target` attribute along with `href="#"`:

```
<div class="dropdown">
  <a class="dropdown-toggle" id="dLabel" role="button"
  data-toggle="dropdown" data-target="#" href="/page.html">
    Dropdown
    <b class="caret"></b>
```

```
    </a>
    <ul class="dropdown-menu" role="menu" aria-labelledby="dLabel">
        ...
    </ul>
</div>
```

Dropdown Usage via JavaScript

To call the dropdown toggle via JavaScript, use the following method:

```
$('.dropdown-toggle').dropdown()
```

Method

The dropdown toggle has a simple method to show or hide the dropdown. There are no options:

```
$().dropdown('toggle')
```

Scrollspy

The Scrollspy plugin (Figure 4-3) allows you to target sections of the page based on scroll position. In its basic implementation, as you scroll, you can add `.active` classes to the navbar based on the scroll position. To add the Scrollspy plugin via data attributes, add `data-spy="scroll"` to the element you want to spy on (typically the body) and `data-target=".navbar"` to the navbar that you want to apply the class changes to. For this to work, you must have elements in the body of the page that have matching IDs of the links that you are spying on.

Figure 4-3. Scrollspy example

Usage

For Scrollspy, you will need to add `data-spy="scroll"` to the `<body>` tag, along with `data-target=".navbar"` that references the element that you are spying on:

```
<body data-spy="scroll" data-target=".navbar">...</body>
```

In the navbar, you will need to have page anchors that will serve as indicators for the element to spy on:

```
<div class="navbar">
  <div class="navbar-inner">
    <div class="container">
      <a class="brand" href="#">Jake's BBQ</a>
      <div class="nav-collapse">
        <ul class="nav">
          <li class="active"><a href="#">Home</a></li>
          <li><a href="#pork">Pork</a></li>
          <li><a href="#beef">Beef</a></li>
          <li><a href="#chicken">Chicken</a></li>
        </ul>
      </div><!-- /.nav-collapse -->
    </div>
  </div><!-- /navbar-inner -->
</div>
```

Usage via JavaScript

If you would rather invoke the scrollspy with JavaScript instead of using the data attributes, you can do so by selecting the element to spy on, and then invoking the .scrollspy() function:

```
$('#navbar').scrollspy()
```

.scrollspy('refresh') Method

When calling the scrollspy via the JavaScript method, you need to call the .refresh method to update the DOM. This is helpful if any elements of the DOM have changed.

```
$('[data-spy="scroll"]').each(function () {
    var $spy = $(this).scrollspy('refresh')
});
```

Options

Options can be passed via data attributes or JavaScript. For data attributes, prepend the option name to data-, as in data-offset="" (see Table 4-3).

Table 4-3. Scrollspy option

Name	Type	Default	Description
offset	number	10	Pixels to offset from top of page when calculating position of scroll.

The offset option is handy when you are using a fixed navbar. You will want to offset the scroll by about 50 pixels so that it reads at the correct time (see Table 4-4).

Event

Table 4-4. Scrollspy event

Event	Description
activate	This event fires whenever a new item becomes activated by the scrollspy.

Toggleable Tabs

Tabbable tabs were introduced in Chapter 3. By combining a few data attributes, you can easily create a tabbed interface (Figure 4-4). To do so, create the nav interface, and then wrap the content of the tabs inside a `<div>` with a class of `.tab-content`:

```
<ul class="nav nav-tabs">
    <li><a href="#home" data-toggle="tab">Home</a></li>
        <li><a href="#profile" data-toggle="tab">Profile</a></li>
        <li><a href="#messages" data-toggle="tab">Messages</a></li>
        <li><a href="#settings" data-toggle="tab">Settings</a></li>
</ul>

<div class="tab-content">
        <div class="tab-pane active" id="home">...</div>
        <div class="tab-pane" id="profile">...</div>
        <div class="tab-pane" id="messages">...</div>
        <div class="tab-pane" id="settings">...</div>
</div>
```

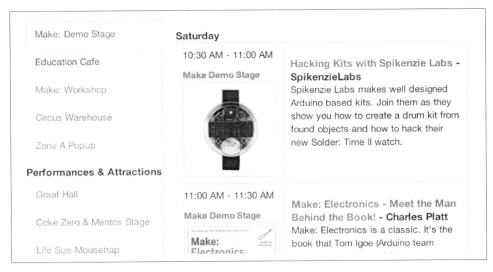

Figure 4-4. Toggleable tabs

Usage

To enable the tabs, you can use the Bootstrap Data API or use JavaScript directly. With the Data API, you need to add `data-toggle` to the anchors. The anchor targets will activate the element that has the `.tab-pane` class and relative ID. Alternatively, `data-target=""` may be used instead of `href="#"` to apply the same action. Here is one way to enable tabs:

```
$('#myTab a').click(function (e) {
        e.preventDefault();
        $(this).tab('show');
})
```

Here's an example of different ways to activate tabs:

```
$('#myTab a[href="#profile"]').tab('show'); // Select tab by name
$('#myTab a:first').tab('show'); // Select first tab
$('#myTab a:last').tab('show'); // Select last tab
$('#myTab li:eq(2) a').tab('show'); // Select third tab (0-indexed)
```

Events

Tabs panes have two different events that can be hooked into, as shown in Table 4-5.

Table 4-5. Toggleable tab events

Event	Description
show	This event fires on tab show, but before the new tab has been shown. Use `event.target` and `event.relatedTarget` to target the active tab and the previous active tab (if available), respectively.
shown	This event fires on tab show after a tab has been shown. Use `event.target` and `event.relatedTarget` to target the active tab and the previous active tab (if available), respectively.

Here's a code example of a shown method:

```
$('a[data-toggle="tab"]').on('shown', function (e) {
        e.target // activated tab
        e.relatedTarget // previous tab
})
```

For information about the `.on` method, refer to the jQuery website (*http://api.jquery.com/on/*).

Tooltips

Tooltips (Figure 4-5) are useful when you need to describe a link or (used in conjunction with the `<abbr>` tag) provide the definition of an abbreviation. The plugin was originally based on the *jQuery.tipsy* plugin written by Jason Frame. Tooltips have since been updated to work without images, animate with a CSS animation, and work with the Bootstrap JavaScript API.

Figure 4-5. Tooltip placement

Usage

To add a tooltip, add `rel="tooltip"` to an anchor tag. The title of the anchor will be the text of a tooltip. The following two examples show how to do this in the Bootstrap Data API and JavaScript, respectively:

```
<a href="#" rel="tooltip" title="This is the tooltip">Tooltip Example</a>

$('#example').tooltip(options)
```

Options

Like all of the plugins, there are options that can be added via the Bootstrap Data API or invoked via JavaScript. All options need to have `data-` prepended to them. So, the `title` option would become `data-title` (see Table 4-6).

Table 4-6. Tooltip options

Name	Type	Default	Description
animation	Boolean	true	Applies a CSS fade transition to the tooltip.
html	Boolean	false	Inserts HTML into the tooltip. If false, jQuery's `text` method will be used to insert content into the dom. Use text if you're worried about XSS attacks.
placement	string/function	'top'	Specifies how to position the tooltip (i.e., top, bottom, left, or right).
selector	string	false	If a selector is provided, tooltip objects will be delegated to the specified targets.
title	string/function	''	The title option is the default title value if the `title` attribute isn't present.
trigger	string	'hover'	Defines how the tooltip is triggered: click, hover, focus, or manually.
delay	number/object	0	Delays showing and hiding the tooltip in ms—does not apply to manual trigger type. If a number is supplied, delay is applied to both hide/show. Object structure is: `delay: { show: 500, hide: 100 }`

Methods

Here are some useful methods for tooltips.

Options

Attaches a tooltip handler to an element collection:

```
$().tooltip(options)
```

Show

Reveals an element's tooltip:

```
$('#element').tooltip('show')
```

Hide

Hides an element's tooltip:

```
$('#element').tooltip('hide')
```

Toggle

Toggles an element's tooltip:

```
$('#element').tooltip('toggle')
```

Destroy

Hides and destroys an element's tooltip:

```
$('#element').tooltip('destroy')
```

Popover

The popover (see Figure 4-6) is a sibling of the tooltip, offering an extended view complete with a heading. For the popover to activate, a user just needs to hover the cursor over the element. The content of the popover can be populated entirely using the Bootstrap Data API. This method requires a tooltip.

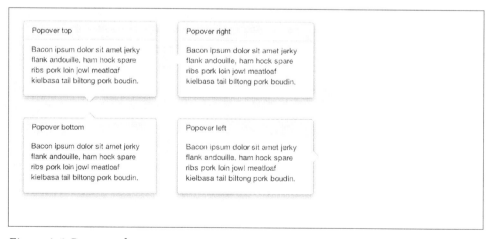

Figure 4-6. Popover placement

Use the following code for popover placement:

```
<a href="#" class="btn" rel="popover" title="Using Popover"
data-content="Just add content to the data-content attribute.">Click Me!</a>
```

Usage

To enable the popover with JavaScript, use the `.popover()` function, passing in any options that you might need:

```
$('#example').popover(options)
```

Options

All options can be passed via the Bootstrap Data API, or directly with JavaScript (see Table 4-7).

Table 4-7. Popover options

Name	Type	Default	Description
animation	Boolean	true	Applies a CSS fade transition to the tooltip.
html	Boolean	false	Inserts HTML into the popover. If false, jQuery's `text` method will be used to insert content into the dom. Use text if you're worried about XSS attacks.
placement	string	function	*right*
Specifies how to position the popover (i.e., top, bottom, left, right)	selector	string	false
If a selector is provided, tooltip objects will be delegated to the specified targets.	trigger	string	*click*
How the popover is triggered (i.e., click, hover, focus, manual)	title	string	function
"	Default title value if *title* attribute isn't present	content	string
function	"	Default content value if *data-content* attribute isn't present	delay
number	object	0	Delays showing and hiding the popover in ms—does not apply to manual trigger type. If a number is supplied, delay is applied to both hide/show. Object structure is: `delay: {show: 500, hide: 100 }`.

Methods

Here are some useful methods for popovers.

Options

Initializes popovers for an element collection:

```
$().popover(options)
```

Show

Reveals an element's popover:

```
$('#element').popover('show')
```

Hide

Hides an element's popover:

```
$('#element').popover('hide')
```

Toggle

Toggles an element's popover:

```
$('#element').popover('toggle')
```

Destroy

Hides and destroys an element's popover:

```
$('#element').popover('destroy')
```

Alerts

With the Data API, it is easy to add dismiss functionality to alert messages (Figure 4-7).

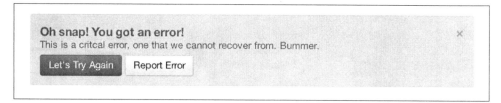

Figure 4-7. Error alert message

Usage

You can close an alert manually with the JavaScript `.alert()` method or use data attributes in conjunction with an anchor or button.

Here is how to dismiss via JavaScript:

```
$(".alert").alert()
```

Here is how to dismiss via Data API:

```
<a class="close" data-dismiss="alert" href="#">&times;</a>
```

Close Method

To enable all alerts to be closed, add the following method. To enable alerts to animate out when closed, make sure they have the `.fade` and `.in` class already applied to them.

```
$(".alert").alert('close')
```

Events

There are two events that can be tied to Bootstrap's `alert` class as shown in Table 4-8.

Table 4-8. Alert class events

Event	Description
close	This event fires immediately when the close instance method is called.
closed	This event is fired when the alert has been closed (will wait for CSS transitions to complete).

As an example, if you wanted to trigger a function after an alert has closed, you could use this function:

```
$('#my-alert').bind('closed', function () {
  // do something…
})
```

Buttons

Buttons were introduced in Chapter 3. With Bootstrap, you don't need to do anything to make them work as links or as buttons in forms. With this plugin you can add in some interaction, such as loading states or button groups with toolbar-like functionality.

Loading State

To add a loading state to a button (shown in Figure 4-8), simply add `data-loading-text="Loading..."` as an attribute to the button:

```
<button type="button" class="btn btn-primary" data-loading-text="Loading...">
Submit!</button>
```

When the button is clicked, the `.disabled` class is added, giving the appearance that it can no longer be clicked.

Figure 4-8. Loading button

Single Toggle

When clicking on a button with the `data-toggle="button"` attribute (Figure 4-9), a class of `.active` is added:

```
<button type="button" class="btn btn-primary" data-toggle="button">Toggle
</button>
```

Figure 4-9. Toggle button

Checkbox Buttons

Buttons can work like checkboxes (as in Figure 4-10), allowing a user to select many of the options in a button group. To add this function, add `data-toggle="buttons-checkbox"` for checkbox style toggling on `.btn-group`:

```
<div class="btn-group" data-toggle="buttons-checkbox">
  <button type="button" class="btn btn-primary">Left</button>
  <button type="button" class="btn btn-primary">Middle</button>
  <button type="button" class="btn btn-primary">Right</button>
</div>
```

Figure 4-10. Checkbox buttons

Radio Buttons

Radio buttons (Figure 4-11) function similarily to checkboxes. The primary difference is that a radio button doesn't allow for multiple selections—only one button in the group can be selected. To add radio-style toggling on btn-group, add data-toggle="buttons-radio":

```
<div class="btn-group" data-toggle="buttons-radio">
  <button type="button" class="btn btn-primary">Left</button>
  <button type="button" class="btn btn-primary">Middle</button>
  <button type="button" class="btn btn-primary">Right</button>
</div>
```

Figure 4-11. Radio buttons

Usage

The .button method can be applied to any class or ID. To enable all buttons in the .nav-tabs via JavaScript, add the following code:

```
$('.nav-tabs').button()
```

Methods

The following methods are useful to use with buttons.

Toggle

Toggles push state. Gives the button the appearance that it has been activated:

```
$().button('toggle')
```

Loading

When loading, the button is disabled and the text is changed to the option from the data-loading-text attribute:

```
<button type="button" class="btn" data-loading-text="loading stuff..." >...
</button>
```

Reset

Resets button state, bringing the original content back to the text. This method is useful when you need to return the button back to the primary state:

```
$().button('reset')
```

String

String in this method is referring to any string declared by the user:

```
$().button('string')
```

To reset the button state and bring in new content, use the string method:

```
<button type="button" class="btn" data-complete-text="finished!" >...</button>

<script>
  $('.btn').button('complete')
</script>
```

Collapse

The collapse plugin makes it easy to make collapsing divisions of the page (see Figure 4-12). Whether you use it to build accordion navigation or content boxes, it allows for a lot of content options.

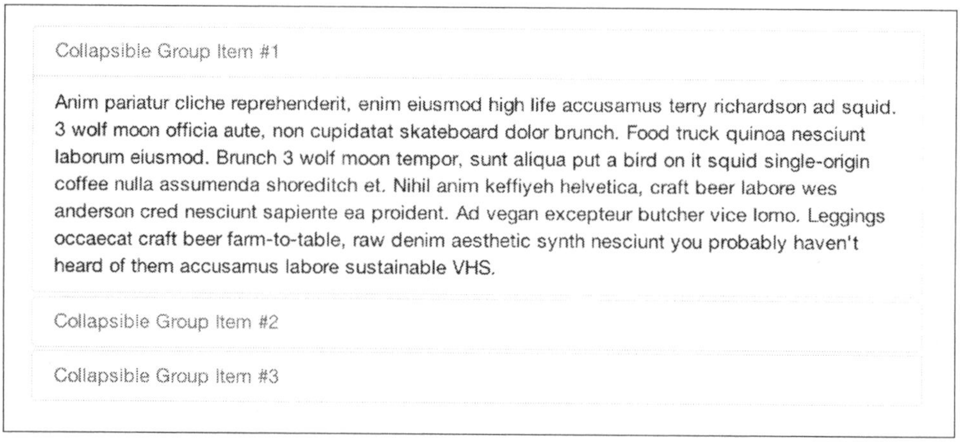

Collapsible Group Item #1

Anim pariatur cliche reprehenderit, enim eiusmod high life accusamus terry richardson ad squid. 3 wolf moon officia aute, non cupidatat skateboard dolor brunch. Food truck quinoa nesciunt laborum eiusmod. Brunch 3 wolf moon tempor, sunt aliqua put a bird on it squid single-origin coffee nulla assumenda shoreditch et. Nihil anim keffiyeh helvetica, craft beer labore wes anderson cred nesciunt sapiente ea proident. Ad vegan excepteur butcher vice lomo. Leggings occaecat craft beer farm-to-table, raw denim aesthetic synth nesciunt you probably haven't heard of them accusamus labore sustainable VHS.

Collapsible Group Item #2

Collapsible Group Item #3

Figure 4-12. Accordion

The following code creates collapsible groups:

```
<div class="accordion" id="accordion2">
  <div class="accordion-group">
    <div class="accordion-heading">
      <a class="accordion-toggle" data-toggle="collapse" data-parent="#accordion2"
      href="#collapseOne">
        Collapsible Group Item #1
      </a>
    </div>
    <div id="collapseOne" class="accordion-body collapse in">
      <div class="accordion-inner">
        Anim pariatur cliche...
```

```
      </div>
    </div>
  </div>
  <div class="accordion-group">
    <div class="accordion-heading">
      <a class="accordion-toggle" data-toggle="collapse" data-parent="#accordion2"
      href="#collapseTwo">
        Collapsible Group Item #2
      </a>
    </div>
    <div id="collapseTwo" class="accordion-body collapse">
      <div class="accordion-inner">
        Anim pariatur cliche...
      </div>
    </div>
  </div>
</div>
...
```

You can also use the data attributes to make all content collapsible:

```
<button type="button" class="btn btn-danger" data-toggle="collapse"
data-target="#demo">
  simple collapsible
</button>

<div id="demo" class="collapse in"> ... </div>
```

Usage

Via data attributes

Like all of the plugins that use the Data API, you can add all needed markup without writing any JavaScript. Add `data-toggle="collapse"` and a `data-target` to the element to automatically assign control of a collapsible element. The `data-target` attribute will accept a CSS selector to apply the collapse to. Be sure to add the class `.collapse` to the collapsible element. If you'd like it to default open, include the additional class `.in`.

To add accordion-like group management to a collapsible control, add the data attribute `data-parent="#selector"`.

Via JavaScript

The collapse method can activated with JavaScript as well:

```
$(".collapse").collapse()
```

Options

The options listed in Table 4-9 can be passed via data attributes or with JavaScript.

Table 4-9. Collapse options

Name	Type	Default	Description
parent	selector	false	If selector, then all collapsible elements under the specified parent will be closed when this collapsible item is shown. (Similar to traditional accordion behavior.)
toggle	Boolean	true	Toggles the collapsible element on invocation.

Methods

The following methods are useful to use with collapsible elements.

Options

Activates your content as a collapsible element. Accepts an optional options object:

```
.collapse(options)
```

Toggle

Toggles a collapsible element to shown or hidden:

```
$('#myCollapsible').collapse({
  toggle: false
})
.collapse('toggle')
```

Show

Shows a collapsible element:

```
.collapse('show')
```

Hide

Hides a collapsible element:

```
.collapse('hide')
```

Events

There are four events that can be hooked into with the collapse plugin, described in Table 4-10.

Table 4-10. Collapse events

Event	Description
show	This event fires immediately when the show instance method is called.
shown	This event is fired when a collapse element has been made visible to the user (will wait for CSS transitions to complete).
hide	This event is fired immediately when the hide method has been called.
hidden	This event is fired when a collapse element has been hidden from the user (will wait for CSS transitions to complete).

After a `<div>` has been collapsed, you could use the following code to execute a function:

```
$('#myCollapsible').on('hidden', function () {
  // do something...
})
```

Carousel

The Bootstrap carousel (Figure 4-13) is a flexible, responsive way to add a slider to your site. In addition to being responsive, the content is flexible enough to allow images, iframes, videos, or just about any type of content that you might want.

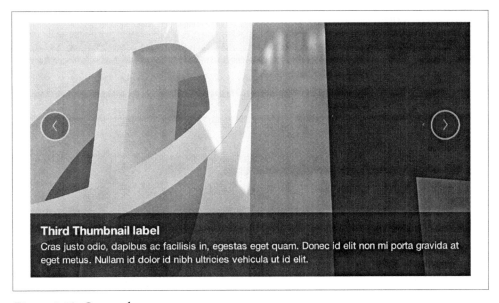

Figure 4-13. Carousel

The following code creates the Bootstrap carousel:

```
<div id="myCarousel" class="carousel slide">
  <!-- Carousel items -->
  <div class="carousel-inner">
    <div class="active item">...</div>
    <div class="item">...</div>
    <div class="item">...</div>
  </div>
  <!-- Carousel nav -->
  <a class="carousel-control left" href="#myCarousel" data-slide="prev">&lsaquo;</a>
  <a class="carousel-control right" href="#myCarousel" data-slide="next">&rsaquo;</a>
</div>
```

Usage

To implement the carousel, you just need to add the code with the markup above. There is no need for data attributes, just simple class-based development. You can manually call the carousel with JavaScript, using the following code:

```
$('.carousel').carousel()
```

Options

Options can be passed through data attributes or through JavaScript. The options are listed in Table 4-11.

Table 4-11. Carousel options

Name	Type	Default	Description
interval	number	5000	The amount of time to delay between automatically cycling an item. If false, carousel will not automatically cycle.
pause	string	"hover"	Pauses the cycling of the carousel on mouseenter and resumes the cycling of the carousel on mouseleave.

Methods

The following methods are useful carousel code.

Options

Initializes the carousel with an optional `options` object and starts cycling through items:

```
$('.carousel').carousel({
  interval: 2000
})
```

Cycle

Cycles through the carousel items from left to right:

```
.carousel('cycle')
```

Pause

Stops the carousel from cycling through items:

```
.carousel('pause')
```

Number

Cycles the carousel to a particular frame (0-based, similar to an array):

```
.carousel('number')
```

Prev

Cycles to the previous item:

```
.carousel('prev')
```

Next

Cycles to the next item:

```
.carousel('next')
```

Events

The carousel has two events that can be hooked into, described in Table 4-12:

Table 4-12. Carousel events

Event	Description
slide	This event fires immediately when the slide instance method is invoked.
slid	This event is fired when the carousel has completed its slide transition.

Typeahead

Typeahead allows you to easily create typeahead inputs in forms (Figure 4-14). For example, you could preload states in a state field or, with some JavaScript, get search results using some AJAX calls.

Figure 4-14. Typeahead

Usage

Using Data API, you can add sources via the `data-source` attribute. Items should be listed in either a JSON array or a function:

```
<input
      type="text"
      class="span3"
      data-provide="typeahead"
      data-items="4"
```

```
data-source="[
        'Alabama',
        'Alaska',
        'Arizona',
        'Arkansas',
        'California',
        ...
        ]"
>
```

To call directly with JavaScript, use the following method:

```
$('.typeahead').typeahead()
```

Options

Table 4-13 shows a list of options.

Table 4-13. Carousel options

Name	Type	Default	Description
source	array, function	[]	The data source to query against. May be an array of strings or a function. The function is passed through two arguments: the query value in the input field and the process callback. The function may be used synchronously by returning the data source directly or asynchronously via the process callback's single argument.
items	number	8	The maximum number of items to display in the dropdown.
minLength	number	1	The minimum character length needed before triggering autocomplete suggestions.
matcher	function	case insensitive	The method used to determine if a query matches an item. Accepts a single argument, the item against which to test the query. Accesses the current query with this.query. Return a Boolean true if query is a match.
sorter	function	exact match, case sensitive, case insensitive	Method used to sort autocomplete results. Accepts a single argument item and has the scope of the typeahead instance. Reference the current query with this.query.
updater	function	returns selected item	The method used to return the selected item. Accepts a single argument item and has the scope of the typeahead instance.
highlighter	function	highlights all default matches	Method used to highlight autocomplete results. Accepts a single argument item and has the scope of the typeahead instance. Should return HTML.

Affix

The affix plugin allows a <div> to become affixed to a location on the page. A common example of this is social icons. They will start in a location, but as the page hits a certain mark, the <div> will become locked in place and will stop scrolling with the rest of the page.

Usage

To apply the affix plugin to a `<div>`, you can use either data attributes, or you can use JavaScript directly. Note that you must position the element so that it can be affixed to the page. Position is controlled by the `data-spy` attribute, using either `affix`, `affix-top`, or `affix-bottom`. You then use the `data-offset` to calculate the position of the scroll.

```
<div data-spy="affix" data-offset-top="200">
        ...
</div>
```

Option

Name	Type	Default	Description
offset	number/ function/ object	10	Pixels to offset from screen when calculating position of scroll. If a single number is provided, the offset will be applied in both top and left directions. To listen for a single direction or multiple unique offsets, just provide an object `offset: { x: 10 }`. Use a function when you need to dynamically provide an offset (useful for some responsive designs).

CHAPTER 5

Using Bootstrap

GitHub Project

Like a lot of great open source projects, the power of Bootstrap comes not just from the developers at the core of the project but also from the development community that supports it. GitHub (*http://github.com*) is a large code repository for projects, and at time of writing, Bootstrap is the most popular project. With over 42,000 stars and over 10,000 forks, the project is bustling with activity. As I mentioned in Chapter 1, if you want to use Bootstrap, you can simply download the *.zip* archive from the site, or you can download using `git`.

For the uninitated, `git` is a free and open source version control system. Bootstrap and a host of other projects manage everything using GitHub, which is an online code repository for `git` projects. To download the source for Bootstrap, run the following commands from the command line:

```
$ git clone https://github.com/twitter/bootstrap.git
```

Cloning Bootstrap will give you a full download of all the files—not just the CSS/Java-Script, but also all of the documentation pages and the LESS files for the dynamic Java-Script elements.

If desired, using the LESS files, you can compile your own version of Bootstrap with the features or customizations that you need.

Customizing Bootstrap

You can download the source, or if you want to easily customize a few of the colors, sizing, or plugins, you can cater the Bootstrap to your needs via the Bootstrap website (*http://twitter.github.com/bootstrap/customize.html*).

When you use the customize page (Figure 5-1), you decide what components you need. For example, you might choose to leave off all of the responsive features, or maybe you would like to leave off the button classes that conflict with styles that you already have. You can also opt out of any of the jQuery plugins. If you know that you aren't going to be using the modals or the carousel, you can leave it out of the build so that you have a smaller file to request.

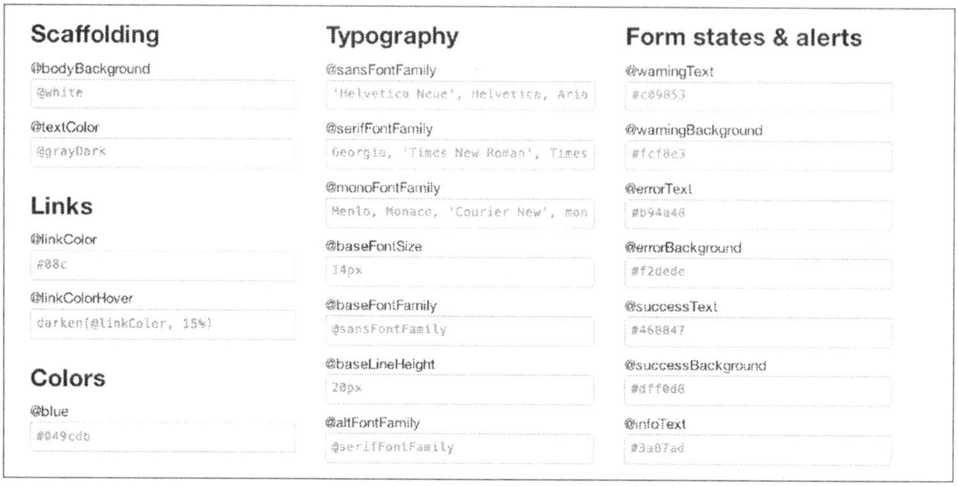

Figure 5-1. Customize page

Lastly, you can configure the LESS variables. Everything from column count to typography colors can be modified here. With these options, you can cater Bootstrap to your needs.

Using LESS

There are a few different ways to use LESS with Bootstrap (Figure 5-2). The first, and perhaps the easiest, is to use a preprocessor like CodeKit (Figure 5-3) or SimpLESS. You can use these tools to watch certain files or folders. Then when you save any of those files, they build the master CSS files. In addition to using traditional CSS techniques, you can use advanced features like mixins and functions to dynamically change the look of your site just by changing some variables.

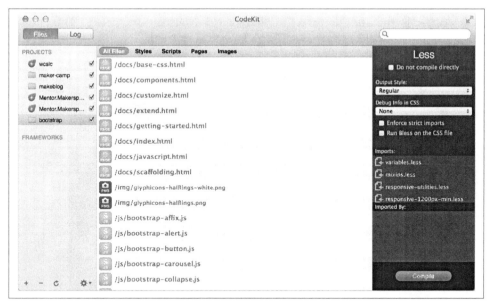

Figure 5-2. Using Bootstrap with LESS

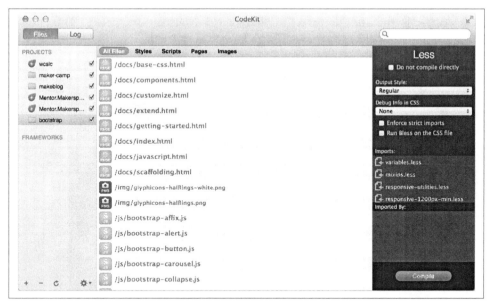

Figure 5-3. CodeKit and the Bootstrap code base

LESS is a dynamic stylesheet language for writing CSS. It allows you to write variables, functions, and mixins for your CSS. The Bootstrap */less/* folder has a few files, but for setting globals, check the *variables.less* and *mixins.less* files.

In the *variables.less* file, you will find all of the global variables for Bootstrap. Let's say you wanted to change the color of all of the links. You would simply update LESS to compile the CSS, and all of the links would change color.

```
/* Old Code */
@linkColor:                    #08c;
@linkColorHover:          darken(@linkColor, 15%);

/* New Code */
@linkColor:                    #7d00cc;
@linkColorHover:          darken(@linkColor, 15%);
```

Now, all links are changed to a purple color, and buttons and other interface elements that call for `@linkColor` will be updated throughout your site.

In the beginning, I was really hesitant to use LESS. After all, I have been writing CSS for a long time, and I didn't feel the need to change. The nesting alone is such a huge timesaver that I'm really glad to have added it to my workflow.

Text Snippets

To rapidly develop Bootstrap sites, I like to use Sublime Text 2 (*http://www.sublime text.com/2*) and the Bootstrap snippets (shown in Figure 5-4) from DEVtellect on Git-Hub (*https://github.com/devtellect/sublime-twitter-bootstrap-snippets/*). This makes adding any component as easy as adding a keyboard shortcut.

Figure 5-4. Bootstrap snippets

To install the snippets, clone the git repository into your packages folder:

```
git clone git@github.com:devtellect/sublime-twitter-bootstrap-snippets.git
```

There are clippings for lots of popular IDEs/text editors.

Photoshop Templates

In addition to snippets, there have been a few Photoshop documents of all of the Bootstrap markup elements. My favorite comes from Repix Design (*http://gui.repixde sign.com/#bootstrap*). Their website is shown in Figure 5-5.

Figure 5-5. Repix design

Here are the features:

- Adjustable colors
- Separate layers
- Vector-based

The PSD is free, but the author requests that you pay with a tweet. Kind of a new spin on the free-as-in-free-speech mantra of open source programming.

Themes

If you have a vanilla installation of Bootstrap, but want to add a bit of panache, there are few different ways to find free, and premium themes for Bootstrap. My two favorites are {Wrap}Bootstrap (*https://wrapbootstrap.com/*), and Bootswatch (*http://boots watch.com/*). Both have some great options, and make it easy to get a new style on your site.

Built with Bootstrap

If you are looking for even more inspiration, check out Built With Bootstrap (*http:// builtwithbootstrap.com/*), a Tumblr that features screen grabs of user-submitted Boot-strap sites. It is a fun way to see the sites using Bootstrap.

Conclusion

As you can see, whatever the project, Bootstrap can fill the needs of just about any Web project. Its blend of responsive framework, extensive JavaScript plugins, and robust interface components make developing easy, fast, and feature rich. It has been great working with Bootstrap over the last year, and I look forward to the future development of the project. Cheers, kudos, and all of the accolades to Jacob Thornton and Mark Otto for creating a project that is so versatile and fun to develop around.

Index

We'd like to hear your suggestions for improving our indexes. Send email to index@oreilly.com.

About the Author

Jake Spurlock is a developer for O'Reilly Media, where he works for *MAKE* magazine. MAKE publishes a DIY magazine, produces Maker Faire, and is trying to turn the world into a better place by teaching people that they can make things. Jake is a Utah native, but a year and a half ago he was grafted into the California wine country.

Colophon

The animal on the cover of *Bootstrap* is the Finnhorse. The Finnhorse is the official horse of Finland, and is nicknamed as the "universal horse" for its ability to meet the agricultural, economic, and recreational needs that a person might require from a horse. Though it has been fully bred and cultivated in Finland for centuries, the exact origin of this horse is unknown.

The vast majority of Finnhorses are a chestnut color, with a very small percentage being black, silver, or bay-colored. In the 1800s, the chestnut-colored Finnhorse only accounted for roughly half the population, but through selective breeding throughout the 19th and 20th centuries, most other genes were bred out, as it was determined that chestnut was the original color of the breed and the national Finnish horse breeding association sought to eliminate "foreign" colors. It was also selectively bred to be an average-sized horse—the average height is 61 inches—with the ability and muscles to do hard labor and the agility to be used for the purposes of riding or entertainment.

Today, most Finnhorses are used for harness racing and other recreational purposes. It was originally the only horse used for racing in Finland, but after the middle of the 20th century, other horses were introduced into the sport. The horse is also used frequently at riding schools and for therapy.

The cover image is from a loose plate of German origin, exact source unknown. The cover font is Adobe ITC Garamond. The text font is Adobe Minion Pro; the heading font is Adobe Myriad Condensed; and the code font is Dalton Maag's Ubuntu Mono.

Get even more for your money.

Join the O'Reilly Community, and register the O'Reilly books you own. It's free, and you'll get:

- $4.99 ebook upgrade offer
- 40% upgrade offer on O'Reilly print books
- Membership discounts on books and events
- Free lifetime updates to ebooks and videos
- Multiple ebook formats, DRM FREE
- Participation in the O'Reilly community
- Newsletters
- Account management
- 100% Satisfaction Guarantee

Signing up is easy:

1. **Go to: oreilly.com/go/register**
2. **Create an O'Reilly login.**
3. **Provide your address.**
4. **Register your books.**

Note: English-language books only

To order books online:
oreilly.com/store

For questions about products or an order:
orders@oreilly.com

To sign up to get topic-specific email announcements and/or news about upcoming books, conferences, special offers, and new technologies:
elists@oreilly.com

For technical questions about book content:
booktech@oreilly.com

To submit new book proposals to our editors:
proposals@oreilly.com

O'Reilly books are available in multiple DRM-free ebook formats. For more information:
oreilly.com/ebooks

O'REILLY®

Spreading the knowledge of innovators | oreilly.com

Have it your way.

CPSIA information can be obtained at www.ICGtesting.com
Printed in the USA
BVOW021437100513

320434BV00003B/3/P